MIND
OVER
MATTER

MIND OVER MATTER

MENTAL HEALTH STORIES
ON COPING WITH STIGMA,
SOCIETY AND SELF

ANTHONY & TYREESE R. MCALLISTER

MIND OVER MATTER
Copyright © 2021 Anthony McAllister and Tyreese R. McAllister
All rights reserved.

Published by Publish Your Gift®
An imprint of Purposely Created Publishing Group, LLC

Unless otherwise indicated, scripture quotations are from the Holy Bible, King James Version. All rights reserved.

Scriptures marked NIV are taken from the New International Version®. Copyright © 1973, 1978, 1984, 2011 by Biblica, Inc.™. All rights reserved.

Scriptures marked NKJV are taken from the New King James Version®. Copyright © 1982 by Thomas Nelson. All rights reserved.

Printed in the United States of America

ISBN: 978-1-64484-335-2 (print)
ISBN: 978-1-64484-336-9 (ebook)

Special discounts are available on bulk quantity purchases by book clubs, associations and special interest groups. For details email: sales@publishyourgift.com or call (888) 949-6228.
For information log on to www.PublishYourGift.com

Table of Contents

Preface

The phrase "mind over matter" references one's ability to use his or her will power to overcome physical limitations. The mind, in and of itself, is capable of overcoming infinite limitations brought on by internal and external forces. Whether the limitations are physical or mental, individuals can allow these forces to prevent them from reaching their full potential.

Despite the fact that mental illnesses are among the most common health conditions in the world, they are among the most stigmatized and discriminated against. Mental illness is characterized as a brain disorder, and diagnoses can include anxiety, bipolar disorder, depression, drug and alcohol addiction, post-traumatic stress disorder (PTSD), schizophrenia, and even grief. Approximately 25 percent of the population experience mental illness in their lifetime, according to the National Association of Mental Illness (NAMI). Similar to other disorders of the body, mental illness can be caused by a variety of factors, such as biological and genetic factors or environmental and social/cultural antecedents. Mental illness symptoms are most often associated with unusual behaviors or bizarre thought disturbances. For the most part, mental illnesses are treatable through psychosocial therapies and medication, allowing those impacted an opportunity to live productive lives. How one deals with his or her disorder can either exacerbate symptoms or enable recovery—though it's important to note that a mental illness is not the person's fault. Unfortunately, stigma and discrimination influence how people deal with their diagnoses.

The stories in this book are of those with lived experiences of dealing with mental health disorders who have decided to overcome and live beyond their diagnoses. These coauthors share their stories of how they have conquered and, in some cases, still work through the intrinsic and extrinsic forces of mental illness, all while establishing a career, going to school, raising children, being married, serving their communities, and living their lives. By sharing their stories, it is their intention to reduce the stigma of mental illness and to encourage individuals impacted by mental health issues to seek treatment and get the necessary support to manage their own mental health.

It does not matter how one arrives at his or her diagnosis—the superpowers are revealed when an individual faces the dark and lonely side of unpleasant and often scary symptoms associated with his or her mental illness. Therefore, it is important for us to believe that it is truly mind over matter, as we are powerful in our determination to overcome.

Good Grief

Tyreese R. McAllister

It's hard to turn the page when you know someone won't be in the next chapter, but the story must go on.

—Unknown Author

"Good grief!" The infamous words of Charlie Brown, often declared by people experiencing a hard time. Had someone asked me if grief could in fact be good, I would have said, "There is nothing good about grief." It's painful. It's heavy. It's never ending—or so it feels. Unlike the Charlie Brown cartoons, grief will not end in thirty minutes when the credits roll. I have to live with this grief for the rest of my life. "Live with" sounds simple, but I more than live with this grief. I carry it everywhere I go. It's the one thing I don't live without. I might forget my iPhone at home and have to go back to retrieve it. I might even walk out the door and forget to grab my purse. But grief—I never get to put it down, let someone hold it for me, or have to return to any place because I left it there. No. Grief is my constant companion.

Twenty-five years of being a mental health clinician and seeing my share of others experiencing grief could not have prepared me for this. Being certified in trauma and helping countless families deal with traumatic events and major losses could not equip me for the murder of my beloved eighteen-year-old daughter Ayana. Breathing is a natural body function that most people never have to practice, but a traumatic experience can literally take your breath away. After the crisis, the grief felt like I was trying to catch my breath. A number of times, I heard a faint voice in my head say, *BREATHE. BREATHE!* This would be followed by a huge inhale and then an exhale. There were times when it felt like I was so oxygen deprived, I had to deeply inhale. There were times when I would follow with exhaling the breath with the same veracity but not much air would come out. I'd wonder, *how long have I not been breathing?* I still find myself, like the Terry McMillan book, waiting to exhale.

When Ayana took her last breath, I was on autopilot, taking care of everything and everybody. I had to make phone calls to people who loved Ayana and our family. Some of these calls could only be made by me. I couldn't have a stranger inform aunts and uncles and cousins that our beloved child had been violently taken away. This was a task that I and I alone had to do. My husband and I both had multiple news interviews. I recall not having the energy to care about what I looked like. *After all, I am a grieving mother,* I thought to myself. My daughter Daja, the diva in the family, was not having it.

"Mom, let me help you," she said.

"I can't! I can't do it," I said, referring to not having any energy to get dressed or argue with her.

"Lollie [what we called Ayana] would not want you to be on television, looking like this."

I chuckled to myself, knowing she was absolutely right. She picked out some clothes, did my makeup, and helped me get dressed.

I stayed busy for the next seven days, doing multiple interviews for each of the major networks and various other media outlets, entertaining family and friends who expressed their condolences in person, checking in on our family, and attending two candlelight vigils. There were hundreds of telephone calls, e-mails, and social media posts to respond to, all while planning a funeral worthy of my princess. Everything had to be just right. The program, the service, the casket, and the horse-drawn carriage, all worthy of our beautiful eighteen-year-old college freshman, who someone violently murdered while she was home on spring break.

Finding an appropriate dress for the princess—something she would like and that was appropriate for her when meeting her Maker—was a challenge. So many people complimented on how beautiful she looked and that her dress was gorgeous. I chuckled to myself every time someone mentioned that dress because I knew that my young adult fashionista would have hated that dress that covered her entire body. Her wardrobe consisted of short shorts, halters, and midriff tops. She was a typical eighteen-year-old who was coming into her own.

After the funeral was over, I had to get my house back in order. Thank God for my sorority sisters, who had been there from the beginning, graciously cleaning, receiving guests, and accepting food, flowers, and other items people brought by. They organized every detail and, most of all, kept me on task. My husband and I had to take our oldest daughter Daja back to college. We had to make sure she was stable enough to be away from home and, for the first time since she was thirteen months old, be without her sister. These two were slightly over a year apart, but they operated more like twins. Daja had been with her sister since she was born. She was the secret keeper and protector of our precious Lollipop.

Just a few months earlier, we were experiencing a mountain high, taking both girls down to Raleigh, North Carolina, as they matriculated to St. Augustine's University, their father's alma mater. Now, here we were, driving only one daughter to school, four hours away from us. We stayed in Raleigh for a few days just to make sure Daja adjusted to what we still refer to as our "new normal." She seemed to be doing well, but it wasn't without some struggles.

Five weeks in, the news media stopped calling for interviews and the company stopped making visits. After we moved Daja back on campus and knew she was settled, Grief moved into our home and remained like an unwelcome visitor that not only wouldn't leave, but seemed to follow me from room to room. I returned to work and tried to get back to my normal routine. As a therapist, I had encouraged many clients to get back to their normal routines as soon as possible, as it is known to help overcome whatever traumatic experience that brought them to therapy. However, there was nothing normal about my life.

That unwelcome guest—Grief—that had shown up at my home on a cool, sunny day in March was also driving with me to and from work. Hell, I think Grief drove the car, 'cause most days, I didn't remember the ride. Grief didn't even have the common courtesy to stay at the house; Grief invited himself to my job. There were days I sat through meetings, and all I remember is the people sounding like the adults in the Charlie Brown cartoons: "Wah, Wah, Wah, Wah, Wah." I tried hard to ignore the fact that Grief was hanging on my neck and taking my breath, but I could not. Grief would not go away or take a break.

Then there were the days when I couldn't bring myself to go to work. I had created an automatic message in my smartphone to text my supervisor, "I'm not coming in today, I'm struggling." He would always reply quickly, "Ok, take care of yourself," as if he too had an automatic reply message. Many days, I couldn't pull myself together to get out of bed. It felt like Grief had sat on my chest and was just too heavy to move. When my husband left for work, I would darken the room and lie there, sometimes all day, with what felt like a weight on my entire body. Me and Grief. Just lying there all day. No television, no music, no scrolling through social media. Nothing. Just me and Grief. I gave myself permission to grieve, to lie in bed, and to feel the loss of her presence.

Into the second month of Grief having moved into my home, I decided to go to a psychiatrist to inquire about something to help me get through those tough days, which seemed to get tougher and tougher. She prescribed Zoloft.

I wasn't surprised it helped, and I was relieved it seemed to kick in so quickly. After a few weeks, I evicted Grief from my residence as I started to get back to myself, the happy-go-lucky, fun-loving, high-energy wife, mother, church member, director, and Delta. I started working on the foundation that my husband, Anthony, and I cofounded in our daughter's name, The Ayana J. McAllister Legacy Foundation, which we established to educate African Americans on how to advocate against gun violence in Black communities. Doing this work helped me get my joy back. I felt alive, I felt energetic, I felt useful and purpose-driven. By shifting my attention away from how awful this situation was for me to how to serve others and fight for community safety and against gun violence helped in ways that can't even be explained.

When faced with a tragedy, people either triumph and rise above or are overcome by their unfortunate circumstances and live a life less than they deserve. What I wanted for myself was what I would have wanted for my own family had it been me who died. I would want them to live on purpose and pursue their dreams. I would not have wanted them to be so overcome with grief that they would defer their dreams, or worse, give up on making a life for themselves.

From the moment my daughters were born, my husband and I had worked with them to prepare them to live without their parents, to be strong, responsible, and independent. It never dawned on me that I would live without either of them. But here I am, once a mother of two beautiful, healthy, and happy daughters, now a mother of one on earth and the other in heaven. This tragedy has changed not only me, but my family. Though my life did not go according to my plan, I still had a life to live. I needed to pull it together and reset. So, reset I did, establishing a nonprofit foundation and a private practice.

I guess Charlie Brown had a point in his exclamation, "Good grief!" I confirmed for myself that being motivated by a tragedy helped me heal and gave me the courage to help others, in a bolder way. I miss my daughter terribly, but I make a conscious decision every day that I will not succumb to the grief that arrived when she left.

Well, this tragedy has changed the trajectory of my life and has defined me. I now use my energy, resources, and yes, even my pain, to help others establish programs and projects that ensure that Black children can grow up in safe neighborhoods.

There is such a huge stigma with mental illness, and many might take issue with grief being considered a mental illness. Regardless of how you look at it, my lived experience with grief told me that I needed an intervention from a psychiatrist to help me take the edge off of the intense emotional pain. Like many other mental illnesses, my grief negatively impacted work, home, and school. I was working on my doctorate when Ayana was killed. I couldn't pull myself up by my bootstraps and get over it. Could I have gotten through without the prescription? Probably. But why suffer needlessly when there is something that can help get through it quicker?

The medication did not remove the grief, but it gave me the kick start I needed to overcome and get my life back on track. I went to work, I got back in school, I started a non-profit foundation, and I opened my private practice. Grief still comes to visit, but it does not stay long. I am too productive to entertain a long visit. I simply sit with Grief for a short while until I let it know, *okay, it's time to go, I have things to do.* Sometimes I sing praise and worship songs at the top of my lungs. It's funny how that drives Grief away. Perhaps Grief doesn't appreciate my off-key singing. Worshiping God also helps me get through.

The presence of Grief is a reminder that I miss my precious princess, Ayana. Think about it—no one grieves anything they didn't love or value. She lived a beautiful life, and someone took it away. That person robbed our family and her friends of a beautiful spirit. They robbed the world of her gracious presence. While I should be outraged that someone would have the audacity to kill my child, my baby girl, my college freshman, I'm not. I forgave the person who stole from me and my family, immediately. There is forgiveness for the person who robbed me of a college graduation, a wedding, and being a grandmother. I forgive the thief who robbed our family of seeing her beautiful smile and enjoying her infectious personality.

Ayana is sorely missed, and my heart is heavy trying to live without her. I still have to remind myself to breathe, to inhale and to exhale. Most days, I function above the grief because she lived, because she loved, and because she is my inspiration to do more for others. The death of a loved one can be overwhelming, but grief can be complicated when the loss is unexpected, at the hand of another, of a child, or self-inflicted.

Give yourself permission to grieve; you need that time. Take the time to process and to cry when you feel like it. You don't have to be a superhero. It's important to allow others to help you and take care of things on your behalf. It's okay to do nothing. If you need help, ask. There are skilled professionals who can assist you through this process with talk therapy, medication, and various other treatment methods. Forgiveness is huge, as it softens the heart and allows the healing to take place, for you. Remember that forgiveness is for you, not the perpetrator. Serving others is also a healing balm, and it gives our lives purpose again.

The Calm Before the Terrifying Storm

Dr. Reneé Allen

As a divorcée-turned-single-mom, I was sometimes so busy in the rat-race routine—trying to make everything work for my son—that I had no clue what was happening before my eyes. I would humbly offer one word of advice when you realize you are dealing with mental illness: patience. According to the *Oxford Dictionary*, patience is "the capacity to accept or tolerate delay, trouble, or suffering without getting angry or upset."

My fifteen-year-old son had been illustrating negative behavior due to many factors: his parents battling through a difficult divorce, the loss of our beautiful home to foreclosure, and my working a stressful job that demanded long hours. His father began distancing himself and was not always available to assist me with our son. My son was very angry at both of us; however, since he lived with me, I was often on the receiving end of his not-so-nice behavior. I initially thought that it was typical teenage behavior, but I eventually learned that it was not.

One day, we went to my son's pediatrician for an unscheduled doctor's visit. As we headed into the exam room, the nurse stopped my son and asked if he wanted to be accompanied by me. She explained to him that he was at an age that I did not have to go into the exam room with him. Initially, this made me uncomfortable; I wished that the nurse would have let me know prior to the visit that she would be making this statement. There was instant thickness in the air. My son chose to go in alone.

According to my son, once he went into the exam room, his pediatrician asked him how things were going at home. This must have been a trigger of some sort for my son, who briskly left the doctor's office. I was oblivious to what was going on until the doctor asked me to come into the exam room. The doctor proceeded to tell me that, based on my son's anger toward me, he believed my life was in danger. I was shocked and overwhelmed to hear those words. All I kept wondering was, what happened in that exam room?

It was as though my son was given some type of false empowerment. My son had entered the doctor's office sad, depressed even, and left the appointment mad, revved up, over the top, and instantly disobedient. For nearly an hour, he would not even get in the car. He was a different person. He did not get what I thought we had come to receive: medical assistance from the doctor who met my son when he was just one day old in the hospital. That day was a critical shift in my son's behavior. I felt like I had been robbed of sharing what had been going on in my son's head, and of participating in his care. That day, I was left alone to navigate my son's mental illness.

We were in the middle of moving, and I had to enroll my son into a new high school, which was public because we could no longer fund a private school education. Little did

I know, the high school that he was to attend was an animal house. The school's guidance counselor was beyond overwhelmed, and it took four or five attempts to finally be able to schedule a parent-teacher meeting. The day that we were scheduled to meet, I planned to leave work and pick up my son from our home. When I arrived to pick him up, he was gone. This marked the first time my son ran away.

The worst feeling that I have ever experienced was having to file a missing person's report after not knowing where my son was for almost two days. I believe that this was the moment I started getting gray hair and the lines on my face. I was overloaded with emotions and worried that my son might have been kidnapped, taken advantage of in some way, or gone for good! I came to find out that he was at his dad's house, and his father chose not to call me. Once my son returned, I was obligated to call an officer to the house to confirm that he was, in fact, home and okay.

Life became a downward spiral. Work became challenging due to my situation at home, and my relationship with my supervisor became challenging. She even questioned whether my son had actually run away. It was the most difficult time of my life, and I received little to no support from my workplace. Both home life and work became a living hell.

After many different challenges with my place of employment, I put in for early retirement. However, what I thought would be a better situation resulted in being rejected by my son. He saw my presence as a way to control him. This devastated me, and our relationship became more difficult. I discovered that he had opened a social media platform and was acting out in a negative way. This was a part of the nightmare. You see, prior to this mental breakdown, my son was a good student: he was well-mannered, was on the math team, played basketball, and was the comedian of the group. Within two weeks of my retirement from the government, my son broke. One day, he stared at me while I was doing paperwork at our dining room table, and then he began mumbling. The next thing I knew, he was throwing empty water bottles and crying uncontrollably.

I called my girlfriend to see if she could recommend a doctor who I could trust, as I had had such a bad experience with my son's pediatrician. She recommended a doctor, who I am indebted to for the rest of my life for helping me get some real help for my son. It was beyond devastating to leave my son in a facility; however, in my gut, I felt I had no other choice.

Even though I was at the facility's mercy, I visited my son every day. I remember my son being so medicated that I cried all the way home, every time I left him. Sometimes he would know that I was there, and more often he would not. It tore me apart, but I knew he needed medical attention. He was never a threat to me; it was more like he was hurting himself emotionally, as though he blamed himself for all that was occurring in our lives. Obviously, he has nothing to do with his dad and my issues. He never even appeared to be suicidal. Unfortunately, for some of the other children on the floor, this was the case, and I cried for them, too.

I felt heavy emotions daily. Mostly, I felt an abundance of guilt. I repeated several what-ifs. What if his dad and I had stayed together and hadn't dragged my son through a bad divorce? What if I hadn't had to take him out of private school and enroll him into a school that, I now know, I would not have left our dog in? What if I hadn't held onto a job that brought me such pain and kept me away from my son? What if, what if, what if—but there is no crystal ball for you to know whether you are making the right decision. I prayed to make the right decisions.

I hope to be a support for the parents and guardians who may not recognize what is going on when an onset occurs in their households. Please don't ask yourself "what if?" Be confident that you are doing the best as humanly possible for your child during these unpredictable times. All the what-ifs did was stall the healing progress and impacted my own mental health; I dealt with my own recurring depression. You cannot push through this in a healthy way if you blame yourself, your spouse, your pediatrician, your family, or anyone else. Be gentle with yourself and your loved ones, who may also be navigating through the drastic and devastating changes. Seek resources and ask people you trust for help.

It's also extremely important to balance what you share with your family and close friends because they also suffer in silence. They may become depressed or frustrated when they are not able to do anything about the situation from afar. For example, after I shared details about my son with my mother and sister, they were overwhelmed with sadness. Honestly, in hindsight, I would not have shared everything with them due to their personal limitations. I found it helpful to talk with professional organizations and groups who were able to relate without being personally impacted.

I pray something in my chapter helped you or will help you, should you find yourself in a similar circumstance in the future. I want all mothers, fathers, guardians, family, and friends to know that it will be alright. Just don't give up on them! Don't leave your child to fend for themselves, or this illness will overtake them. It is not easy, but embracing your new normal can make a big difference in the recovery and healing process.

In my humble opinion, I feel that each of us experiences mental illness and we have a breaking point. Once a human being "breaks," they need love, support, medical treatment, and prayer so that everyone has an opportunity to WIN! They don't need for you to feel sorry for them. The stigma must end because mental illness and post-traumatic stress disorder (PTSD) is now a part of everyone's life. We must recognize it, seek help, and take it day by day! By His Grace and Mercy, I am doing it and you can, too! God bless you and your family always! In Jesus' name, Amen!

Struggling While Serving

Mark T. Gibson

If you are a pastor of a very progressive church, you may experience times when the demons are not in the pews, but rather they are possessed within your own personality. I struggled with a bout of depression in 2018, which caused me to tender my letter of resignation to my board of directors. This was not because of some juicy scandal that I, the pastor, had been caught up in or an act of mutiny from the congregation. No—this letter was simply stating, "I have had enough!" I had hit the proverbial wall and did not know how to handle this looming cloud that hung over my head and life. My church was thriving, our financials were excellent, and the reputation of the church was resounding throughout the city, so the ultimate question was, "What seems to have been the problem?" It was the enemy within me that had ignored the success God had granted our ministry. In this chapter, I will give you insight into what appears to be a glorious and popular position in the church that can have poisonous leaves attached to it. I will discuss the struggles, sidetracks, and situational walls that many pastors and servant leaders experience and refuse to admit and seek help for: pastoral depression.

As a young boy growing up in Washington, DC, I was always excited when Ringling Bros. and Barnum & Bailey Circus came to the DC Armory. My mom and aunt would take my twin brother and me to see the sites and sounds of The Greatest Show on Earth. I was fascinated by the pageantry and precision of the various acts, from the ringmaster's deep baritone voice to the flying trapeze. The costumes and lights captivated me for the whole two hours we sat in our seats. And there was one specific act that totally mesmerized me: the juggling. Oh, how this guy would juggle balls and knives and even chainsaws, hoping that he would never drop anything he threw into the air.

"Wow, how does he do that?" I would ask.

Year after year, my mother would whisper to me, "Mark, he does it so well because he concentrates on one spot in the air and never loses his focus."

Little did I realize that she was prophesying into my life what I would ultimately be faced with as a pastor: juggling.

My story of struggling with mental health issues dates back to May 1992 when I worked as an on-air personality for a local university's radio station. I had known something was wrong because at my 7:30 a.m. bottom-of-the-hour-segment, I had a strange feeling come over me that caused me to become very lethargic. Then a knock on the station door led to the news that my identical twin brother had passed away. My best friend drove me home to prepare to leave for Washington, DC.

I had seen my twin brother in Washington, DC, just weeks before. He had really not wanted me to return to Danville, Virginia, so he decided to recite the chant from *The Color Purple*: "You and me must never part . . . Mocky Da-Da."

This chant may seem silly to some, but for me, the scene of Celie and Nettie making a pact to always remain bonded and connected became our way of expressing the love and dedication that would never end between us. Now he was gone. There would be no more weekly calls, no more silly outings, no more jokes about relationships.

One of my brother's last requests was about visiting my first-born son, who was to be born in November. It was my brother's desire to make certain that my son was dressed in the outfits that he had purchased for him prior to him leaving the hospital so that he would make a fashion statement in that "country hick town of Danville, VA, that you live in."

My life would change drastically, and yet I never took the time to process the loss of a person who I spoke to every week of my life for twenty-seven years. My twin brother was gay and had contracted AIDS. It was difficult to see him dwindle away in front of our eyes. I loved him more than life itself. To all of us, he was our brother, our son, our friend.

Sitting in the church at his funeral, I kept a stiff upper lip and did not shed one tear in public. The good son that I was, I adhered to the instructions of my family. Showing this type of emotion would show that we were not accepting God's Will. Expressing sorrowful emotions was also a display that we had not shown love for the deceased while they lived; therefore, I had to remain strong for those who were not as strong during this time of death. I internalized my hurt and pain and shared my reflections about the one person in the entire world who I not only looked like, but admired for all of the obstacles that we had overcome together.

Fast forward to September 10, 1998, I was engaged in a staff meeting at the college I worked for in the hills of Virginia. I served as the director of residence life and had the staff there to congratulate them for a job well done during a smooth check-in and transition process with our students. My phone rang, but I refused to allow anything to interrupt my conversation with the staff. My secretary was feverishly calling and instant messaging me to get my attention for an emergency call that she had received from my family. Finally, she interrupted the meeting by walking into the meeting room to alert me that there was a call I needed to take immediately. Tears were running down her face, and I could not understand why.

"Is this Mark Gibson?" the person asked on the other end of the phone.

I confirmed it, and the person announced that I needed to get back to Danville.

"There has been a terrible accident, and one of your sons has been injured in the car accident."

I had two sons at this time and kept asking which one of my sons. They could not tell me, but I needed to get to Danville quickly. The drive from Ferrum, Virginia, to Danville was at least an hour and a half. I made it in fifty minutes. I arrived at the hospital's emergency department and was met by a family friend who immediately grabbed me and embraced me and kept saying "I am so sorry."

"Sorry for what . . . which one is hurt?"

They carried me back to see my oldest son, my name-sake, stretched out on a gurney with a halo attached to his neck and head. I saw a little trickle of blood coming down the side of his mouth, and I prayed to God to raise my son off that bed. It did not happen. He died from an airbag deploying and snapping his neck. It was instant.

My twin brother was gone and now my oldest son. *God, what are you doing in my life? I have been serving and faithful to you. You called me into ministry over four years ago, and now this?* It had been my son's first day of attending elementary school, which he referred to as "Big School" since he had been attending preschool and daycare. That morning, he had promised to tell me all about his day when I got home. Now I was faced with not hearing about his classmates or teachers but making funeral arrangements for an angel among humans.

Once again, at his homegoing celebration, the expectation was to not display any emotions and to remain strong for the family to show the acceptance of the Will of God for my son's life. Of course, I complied and did my best to comfort my wife and son because I was not only the head of my house, but I was a called man of God. The college where I worked shut down to come and attend the service, and just about everyone in the city packed the church. Everything was a haze for me, but I remember my bishop talking about David losing his son and eventually getting up and going to worship and then having another child.

My wife would give birth to our third child less than two years later, but five years following his birth, I would transition into divorce and lose custody of my sons. Times were rough for me. I left the home with one set of bedroom furniture and my clothes. I was pastoring my first church, and many of my congregants did not understand how a pastor could lead them and leave his own home. The clouds were looming, but I managed to find a ray of sunshine with eventually meeting my new wife.

She was not only a great listener, but she motivated me to look past the disappointments of my past experiences of loss to find the true passion for my purpose in life, to embrace tragedies and setbacks and use them as springboards to greater things to come in my future. We married in March 2009 and relocated to Raleigh, North Carolina. I had hit the reset button on life. This new life felt spectacular with the love of my life, in a different location, and with a new job at a local community college. For nine years, life seemed to be operating smoothly, without any signs of complications from the pains of my past.

It was Thanksgiving 2018. The ministry was going well, but I was not in the typical festive mood. My second wife's family had noticed that I was not my usual jovial self. I was very reserved, and at times, I removed myself from the celebration. I assured everyone that I was fine, only tired from the load of being bivocational. Christmas came and went, and I was still not myself. I sat down with my wife and announced I was done with ministry. I had had enough of the constant pulling and tugging; the juggling act was not working for me any longer. I had "dropped the ball" because I was no longer engaged or able to concentrate on my assignment.

I wrote my letter of resignation and called my leadership team and board of directors into my office at the New Year's Eve service to announce I was resigning. They wore shock and surprise on their faces as they asked if it was something that the church had done. The finances and membership were growing by leaps and bounds, and yet I was ready to leave. I assured them all that the church was not at the root of my decision; I just did not want to do "this" any longer. My chairman of deacons excused everyone from the meeting and pleaded with me to take some time off and reevaluate after a two-month sabbatical. I agreed to the time off with one stipulation: "Do not send any church folk by the house to pray for me, no scriptures read to me, no phone calls to check on me, nothing!"

Three days later, two couples who were church members and friends of ours stopped by the house to see us. I gave my wife the side-eye while I sat in my man cave at home, pissed off that she let them in the door. But they had come to encourage me, not to sit in my pity, not to allow my misery to become my ministry. One of the ladies got her girlfriend on the phone for me to talk with who had suffered a great loss in her life. This person introduced me to a therapist, who I connected with immediately.

He did not want to talk with Pastor Gibson; he wanted to talk with Mark. This was a great start for me because he knew nothing about me or my church. He knew I was a pastor but had no idea where I pastored. He was a pastor also and therefore would be able to identify with the struggles and work of the position without me having to provide detailed information about the vocation of pastoring. I would eventually begin to travel back to the Washington, DC, area each week to meet with this therapist, who would not only change my life, but save it.

Though my therapist is a pastor himself, his practice is not a church service or Bible study. He could not understand how I was able to remain so functional in my role as pastor, husband, father, grandfather, son, brother, dean of students, community activist, and student. I was able to be transparent, and he gave me permission to do something I had not done. He allowed me to grieve the loss of my twin and my son. I had suppressed twenty-six years of grief within myself, and it had come back to haunt me in a major fashion. I was diagnosed as clinically depressed.

"DEPRESSED?" I asked in shock. "I am not depressed, fed up maybe but definitely not depressed, Doc!"

I was asked a pivotal question during my very first session: "When was the last time you cried about your twin and your son?" I could not answer, and my therapist allowed me to do what I was told was a sign of weakness—something that my family never did in public. I had the best cry since I was a baby. He showed me how cluttered my brain was with all my issues; the remaining 5 percent was trying to overcompensate to cover for the 95 percent that was overwhelmed.

It was a cleansing that I needed, it was a connection that I admired, it was a conversation that I deserved.

Who helps the healer when he or she is wounded? Too many of us as clergy tend to wear that S on our chest and feel that we show weakness should we not perform in the role of pastor twenty-four hours a day, seven days a week. We fall into the misguided and erroneous doctrine that, because of our connection to God, there is no way we should suffer with any type of mental struggle or illness. The stigma assigned to this topic, particularly in the African American community, has kept so many from getting the necessary help for their families and community. It is my personal belief that if anyone pastors African American folk, you *need* a therapist because we are often the dumping grounds for everyone's problems and therefore have no space for our own.

We have become creatures of camouflage, masters of masquerade, and deflectors of our own disappointments. When it comes to ourselves, we cling to the minimum and neglect our needs, yet we give so much to everyone else. I suffered from compassion fatigue where, for years, my congregation, family, community, friends, and associations had all gotten the best of me except me. Self-care is vitally important, particularly with pastors, and we must be unapologetic about taking time to reset. We can minister to others from a wounded place but never from a broken place in life.

Too many of us try to lead while on empty, and we stall on the road of life because we have focused on others instead of stopping and refueling. This was brought to light one year when my wife and I took a flight to a tropical vacation. As we sat on the plane ready to take off, the flight attendant reminded us that, should the cabin lose pressure, oxygen masks would fall from the ceiling: "Before you administer oxygen to anyone else, first administer it to yourself." What an awesome message to pastors, leaders—anyone. We are no good to anyone else until we are first good to ourselves. Remember, even the juggler at the circus does not juggle during the entire performance. He or she has only one set and then, once it is over, takes a break and rests. If Jesus could take a break and get away, why should we not do the same to maintain our peace and balance? Mental wellness is not only precious, it is necessary.

Choosing Faith Over Fear

Lee R. Jackson

I am not who anxiety says I am.
I am who God knows I am.

I sat in stunned silence, desperately trying to process the information that I had just received. I was quiet for what seemed like an eternity. Finally, I asked the doctor to repeat what he had just told me: "Lee, you have a panic disorder."

The doctor continued, "A panic disorder is basically when your body's natural alarm system goes off at the wrong time. The fight or flight response is triggered even when there's no real danger. Your heart rate increases, your muscles tense up, your blood pressure elevates, in addition to any number of other physical symptoms that are caused by the release of cortisol and adrenaline into the bloodstream."

"Why me?" I asked.

"Well," he replied, "some people are just more sensitive to stress. And based on what you told me you've been going through over the past few years, it's no surprise that your stress levels are through the roof."

He was referring to the fact that I had lost both of my parents to cancer just two and a half years apart. And he was right. It was excruciatingly painful and stressful.

Two months after my mom's funeral, I was rushed to the hospital with what I thought was a heart attack. But after a thorough check-up, I was given a clean bill of health. After several more false alarms, someone recommended that I see a therapist because they believed my problem might be stress-related. And sure enough, it was. Those physical symptoms that I thought were heart attacks were actually panic attacks.

You would've thought that I'd be relieved to find out that I didn't have a heart condition. Nope. I was actually disappointed. There was a part of me that would've rather had a physical health problem than a mental health problem. All I could think was, *people are going to think I'm "crazy."* I was ashamed and embarrassed.

In retrospect, I realize how wrong I was. I understand now that mental health challenges are nothing to be ashamed of or embarrassed about. But that just goes to show how powerful the stigma is. I was diagnosed with a panic disorder way back in 1992, when the stigma was even worse. We've come a long way since then, but we've still got a long way to go. Our work won't be done until we live in a world where mental health is discussed openly and honestly as a regular part of life.

If you're suffering from anxiety and panic attacks, please speak to a mental healthcare professional. Don't put it off. Removing the stigma begins by changing one mind at a time. And all change begins with you. Show the world that you aren't embarrassed by your mental health challenges. Share your truth with the world. Don't be afraid of people judging you. There's nothing more empowering than being your authentic self.

I say this based on my own experience. I believe my recovery from anxiety took much longer than it needed to because I was afraid to tell people about my panic disorder. I was so worried about people seeing me have a panic attack that I became agoraphobic. Agoraphobia is when your anxiety is so bad that you're actually too scared to leave the house. I constantly turned down social engagements for fear of having a panic attack. I made up a lot of excuses. In other words, I lied. A lot. It was exhausting. And I felt horrible about lying to my friends. This led to more stress, which of course led to—yup, you guessed it—more anxiety. And the cycle continued on an endless loop.

I'm writing this chapter because I don't want you to make the same mistakes that I made. To steer you in the right direction, here are my top three steps that every anxiety sufferer should follow.

1) Educate Yourself

Knowledge is powerful. The more you know about anxiety, the better equipped you'll be to overcome it. The best way to begin is by booking an appointment with a mental health professional who specializes in anxiety. At the appointment, ask a lot of questions. Use the time to start learning about the biology of anxiety. In other words, find out what's happening in your body when you're having an anxiety attack. Being well informed about the topic makes it far less intimidating. At least half of the terror of an anxiety attack stems from the fear of the unknown. Your heart starts pounding, and you immediately start freaking out, thinking, *Oh my God! What's happening to me? Is it a heart attack? Am I dying?* Removing the guesswork is a game changer. When you know what to expect, you can mentally prepare for it. Eventually, you'll begin to say to yourself, *I recognize this feeling. I'm uncomfortable, but I'm not in danger.* That's a huge step on your road to recovery.

Your response to the initial physical symptoms won't exacerbate the symptoms like it has in the past. You can break the typical pattern. Here's the typical pattern that most anxiety sufferers can relate to: fight or flight response kicks in à your body releases stress hormones into your bloodstream à your physical symptoms emerge à you overreact to those symptoms à BAM! your body releases even more stress hormones, and your symptoms get more severe. When you don't overreact to the physical symptoms, you can break the pattern. How do you do that? By acknowledging the symptoms but not dwelling on them. Recognize the difference? This small behavioral shift can influence the length and severity of a panic attack.

Speaking of behavioral shifts, that brings me to a little thing called cognitive behavioral therapy, also known as CBT. This is the number one most commonly used talk therapy for anxiety. I highly recommend that you pursue it with your chosen mental health professional. It has a great track record for producing results in overcoming not only anxiety, but depression, eating disorders, and post-traumatic stress disorder. CBT helps you to become aware of negative thinking patterns and teaches you to deal with stressful situations in a constructive way. It's a great tool to have in your box. For some people, it's the only tool they need to overcome anxiety. For others, like me, it was one of the many tools necessary to become anxiety free. I also used (and continue to use) stress reduction practices like mindfulness meditation, breathing exercises, and my number one favorite tool, which I'll tell you about later in this chapter.

We live in a time when all of the information in the world is only a Google search away. Keep educating yourself about all of the anxiety-fighting strategies available out there, and be sure to research and read about other people's challenges with anxiety. Remind yourself that there are millions of people suffering from anxiety just like you are. That will help to keep you from feeling isolated and alone. Finding and joining a support group will help even more. You've got a lot of options.

2) Educate Your Friends and Family

Explain to your loved ones what anxiety is and what you're going through. Be completely transparent with them. Tell them how common it is. Give them all of your newly learned statistics. Most people who have never experienced anxiety have no idea what it's like or what causes it. They're likely to have wildly inaccurate theories.

Your loved ones will be grateful that you shared your challenges with them. And the millions of anxiety sufferers in the world should be grateful for your transparency as well. Why? Because you have created more awareness about the subject of mental health. Your loved ones will take their new knowledge and empathy into the world. Conversations will take place. Minds will change. A ripple effect will occur, caused by your honesty. That's how we remove the stigma. Inch by inch. Step by step. One honest conversation at a time.

3) Choose Faith Over Fear

My life profoundly changed when I made the conscious decision to wake up every morning and choose faith over fear. Before I made that decision, fear was the boss. Fear ran the show. But everything changed on a Saturday morning in 1994.

My anxiety was so bad that I hadn't left the house in days. This agoraphobia led to severe depression. I couldn't eat. I couldn't sleep. I refused to see any of my friends. I didn't answer the door or the telephone for days. I didn't want anyone to see me like this. As I got more and more depressed, I started thinking about my older brother who had committed suicide when I was eight years old. It suddenly dawned on me that maybe my brother had felt the same way I do. Maybe he had debilitating anxiety, just like me, and maybe that's why he killed himself. Tears rolled down my face as I dropped to my knees and began to pray. I said, *God. Please help me.*

I don't want to die. But I can't live like this. Please help me. I need a miracle.

Two seconds later, the phone rang. Even though I hadn't answered the phone in days, I figured I'd better answer it because, well, when you pray for a miracle and the phone rings, you should probably answer it. So I did. It was my friend Breanna. She was one of only a couple of friends who knew about my anxiety. She insisted that I get out of the house and spend the day with her, visiting yard sales and flea markets. She also said that she wouldn't take no for an answer. She was shocked by how quickly I agreed.

Breanna picked me up promptly at noon, and off we went. When we got to the first yard sale, there was nothing but furniture: chairs, tables, couches, shelves, and desks. Then there was one book. It looked totally out of place all by itself among the furniture. One little lonely book lying on a towel by the antique rocking chairs. It was an old, stained, dog-eared paperback with a sticker pronouncing its cost to be 75 cents.

I picked it up and read the cover: *Creative Visualization: Use the Power of Your Imagination to Create What You Want in Your Life* by Shakti Gawain. I looked up at the sky and smiled from ear to ear. I knew. I just knew. Me finding this book was not a coincidence. I couldn't wait to get home and dig into it.

After a few more stops and a bite to eat, Breanna dropped me off. I gave her a big hug and thanked her for being such a good friend. We both teared up a little. Happy tears. I ran into the house and found a comfy spot to settle in and devour my book. After only a few pages, I knew that this book was exactly what I needed. It was speaking directly to my soul. Definitely the best 75 cents I have ever spent. After I read it once, I read it a second time, armed with a highlighter so I could highlight all of my favorite parts and put the methods into action the next morning.

This miraculous book was the beginning of my spiritual journey. It also put me on the road to recovery from my anxiety disorder. It opened up the floodgates. I immersed myself in dozens and dozens of spiritual books. My life was forever changed.

I prayed for a miracle and I got one. From that moment on, faith became my default setting. So you may have figured out that my number one tool against anxiety is . . . ta-da! Visualization. Once I mastered the art of visualization, my anxiety subsided almost immediately. If you've never heard of visualization, the best way to describe it is mental rehearsal. All elite athletes do it in one form or another. They picture themselves catching the winning touchdown or hitting the game-winning homerun. They mentally rehearse it so many times that it feels like it's already happened before the game is even played. Another way to describe visualization is deliberate daydreaming. Everyone daydreams, but visualization is like daydreaming with a purpose. You pick the topic and the outcome.

I started visualizing myself as being totally relaxed and calm before I left the house. I did it over and over until my subconscious mind was convinced that I was relaxed and calm. Instead of imagining the worst-case scenario (anxiety) and bringing it to fruition, I imagined the best-case scenario. It worked. And all these years later, it still works.

Visualization allows you to keep choosing faith. The ultimate faith is seeing yourself the way that God sees you. Once you start seeing yourself the way that God sees you and start loving yourself the way that God loves you, anxiety doesn't stand a chance.

Close your eyes. Relax. Picture the best version of yourself. How does that version of you walk? How does that version of you talk? How does that version of you smile? How does that version of you make others feel? That best version of you is the real version of you. Remember that. Keep choosing faith.

Living with a Stranger

Charles Louis Lee Jr.

Forty-one years and counting, I live with a stranger who scares me. I never know what he is capable of, and I struggle to keep him under control. That stranger is depression.

As a young child, I always felt loved by my parents. They made me feel comfortable. I always felt safe. I knew with them around, nothing would happen to me. All that security changed in 1979 when my parents separated. They made great attempts at co-parenting, but their own fights with their depressive disorders made it almost next to impossible to include me in their world. The more they struggled, the more forgotten I felt. As a child, I could never express what I was feeling because I didn't understand what was transpiring. I watched my parents argue and fight prior to separation, and because it happened so often, it became part of my norm. I would hide in my bedroom and wait for the storm to pass.

After their separation, the storms ended and my new norm was living primarily with Mom and visiting Dad on weekends when possible. I wasn't the traditional child who gravitated toward same-aged children. I gravitated toward adults because I was always a curious person and wanted to learn. I wanted to grow up quickly. I didn't realize just how quickly I actually would.

In September of 1981, I had my first unsuspected experience with depression. My father became extremely depressed over the separation of him and my mother. He wouldn't eat, work, or do anything to care for himself. I hadn't seen or spoken with my father for several months, as he hadn't wanted me to see him in his current condition. My mother did her best to explain what was happening, but it wasn't making sense to a ten-year-old.

On November 23, 1981, my father took his life in the most horrific fashion. He stood in front of a moving train and succumbed to his injuries. He left this world without any explanation—and that is when I was greeted by this stranger I didn't understand. The stranger manifested himself in my dreams. I experienced a series of unexplainable night terrors. Along with the night terrors came unexplainable crying fits. I fell into a deep depression over the loss of my father. I was a recluse for months. No interactions with childhood friends. No energy. No behaviors you would expect from a ten-year-old boy. I received no support from my mother, who clearly didn't notice the changes in my behavior. The night terrors appeared to be more of an irritant to her than a sign there was a problem with her child. That's when I realized I was living with a new stranger. This stranger I called "Mother."

I had always viewed my mother as a strong Black woman who was invincible. There was nothing she couldn't do in my eyes. This was a woman who I relied on to care for me and help make my dreams come true. It was a surprise to learn she wasn't as invincible as I thought. My mother began to manifest her own demons as a result of my father's passing. Her behaviors would change day to day, sometimes hour to hour. Sometimes I found myself afraid. Sometimes I didn't know who she was. She began to drink alcohol and smoke marijuana.

By the time I was twelve years old, her substance abuse became obvious and excessive. This is when my childhood ended and my adulthood began. I found myself having to be the parent and having to raise myself. I began to lean on my maternal family for help. I feared what would happen if left to the task of caring for my mother by my lonesome. Confused and unaware of what I was dealing with, I feared losing her.

It was assumed Momma was just a substance abuser. My family did the best they could in supporting me since this was a disease they had fought and some had won. They gave me advice as to what I needed to do in support of my mother.

As the years progressed, my mother's stranger still had no name. I would find liquor bottles stashed all over the apartment. She began to hide alcohol from me to keep me from getting rid of the bottles. I would make urgent pleas to my mother and explain how her behaviors were making me feel. But to no end. My mother continued to drink, smoke, and sleep. It amazed me how she managed to function at her full-time job but then come home and turn into a nightmare.

I then discovered Momma had started taking diet pills. I didn't understand the reasoning, and when I inquired, I was reminded to stay in a child's place. As the stranger contin-ued to manifest himself within my mother, things got worse. When I was around the age of twelve or thirteen, my mother began mixing alcohol and pills. There were three occasions when she overdosed, and I had to rush her to the hospital. While she was in the hospital, I was left to fend for myself. Because I had been such an inquisitive child. I had learned from my mother during her moments of stability.

My mother continued this spiral for a number of years. Her behavior manifested to poor decision-making, promiscuous behaviors, and public outbursts. It wasn't until—finally—an emergency room doctor recognized her symptoms from her multiple ER visits that she was diagnosed with bipolar disorder with psychotic features. She began a course of outpatient treatment that began to give me some normalcy in my life. I finally thought I was getting back the woman I knew and loved in my early childhood years. Yes, Momma was cured—or so I thought.

As my mother was engaging in her treatment, I didn't realize how much I was going to be a part of her success. Attending family therapy sessions, learning about her medications, learning to recognize changes in her behavior that would suggest a probable relapse—it became too much for a kid. Even with the family's support, I became the sole care provider. Anger and sadness set in for me. My stranger continued to form. I found myself starting to resent my mother because although we never talked about my father's death, as I got older, it became very obvious to me what he had done to himself. I attempted to mourn his death for years, constantly trying to understand why and wondering what it meant for me. To this day, I have never been angry with my father for what he did, which is something that has always puzzled me.

I had developed a trick called thought suppression, which allowed me to hide my pain and maintain focus on caring for my mother and keeping our family together. Although she was now attending outpatient psychiatric treatment and NA and AA meetings, my mother still struggled with periodic relapses and still needed me for support. I managed to fight through the resentment and continued to help my mother through her struggles.

At age fifteen, things were still fairly status quo but better. My mother had a number of psychiatric inpatient stays, and through these visits, I learned about bipolar disorder. I needed to know about my mom's condition in order to better support her. I learned her medications, I learned about side effects, and most importantly, I learned about the signs and symptoms of decompensation, the process of mental health deteriorating. In effect, I became an expert on my mom. When I thought things were getting better, I took on a part-time job. Surprisingly, I was doing well in school, and my schoolteachers, not knowing my deep dark secret, saw a flourishing and happy child.

During the summer of 1987, things began to take a turn for the worse. The substance abuse started again, which led to more inpatient hospitalizations. Mom's behavior began to threaten our way of living. She was taking off from work more, threatening our survival. We managed to avoid eviction a number of times. I knew I had to make a decision that would change the course of my future but would inevitably save my family.

In the spring of 1988, I found myself having a discussion with my school guidance counselor to announce my dropping out of school. Naturally, she was disappointed—and even more disappointed when I was unwilling to share the reason. I had already weighed the pros and cons of the risks I'd be taking sharing my home life with my counselor. I was afraid my sharing would lead to the separation of my family. My part-time job turned into a full-time job in order to help support my family. I did all this unbeknownst to my mother. My mother was so separated from my life, she had no idea I was no longer attending school.

Things started to get better; however, we continued with our good months and bad months. I became the full-time adult. I made sure the bills got paid, ensured medication compliance, and ran interference with her job to help her maintain employment. I had to become a liaison between my mother and her supervisor to conceal her illness. This went on for three more years until Momma was finally on a regimen that kept her stable. Normalcy returned, but at that point, I really didn't know what normal was.

I finally was able to move away from home in 1991. I then began to manifest signs and symptoms of what I thought was bipolar behavior. My behaviors were trending similar to Momma's. I began to lash out at friends and colleagues at work. On occasion, my attitude began to border on insubordinate toward my work supervisor. At the time, I was working in an acute psychiatric hospital where I made the care of patients my top priority. I found it easy to help others, but I was unable to help myself. My crying spells returned. I found myself reliving my childhood through night terrors. I found myself feeling depressed on days at a time. I was finally forced by my employer to seek treatment because I was told I presented a danger to others. I sought out my own health professional and began seeing a clinical/forensic psychologist twice weekly.

I learned a lot about myself. I discovered the reason for my pain and depression, and that suppressing my pain was dangerous, even though it was how I managed. After the first year of treatment, I was diagnosed as a clinical depressant. I was relieved to learn I had a mendable condition. According to my doctor, because I never properly grieved for the death of my father and ultimately found myself caring for my only living parent, I became resentful and easily agitated toward others. I was lashing out at individuals who were genuinely trying to offer help, but I saw their concern as judgment. These behaviors were brewing in my subconscious, and I used this as a reason to make verbal attacks.

I began a course of antidepressants, which I complied with for a little while, but after six weeks, I chose to stop taking them because of the physical side effects. I didn't initially share this information with my physicians, but once they were informed, they warned me of the consequences of noncompliance. I decided to accept the responsibility of not taking the medication, against my psychologist's suggestion. I found that talking through my issues helped me. I found that sharing my story with others in need helped me.

Now, at age forty-nine, I reflect on my life and it's direction. I've been driven to serve what I call my community. I have experienced quite a few setbacks. I attempted suicide after the loss of my six-year-old son in 2006. I struggled back from a deep depression by returning to the one professional field that gave me promise: mental health. My mother resorted back to her old ways. I continued to provide her support until her passing in February 2017. To this day, I struggle with the stranger. I now deal with florid suicidal ideations with no real plan to execute. I'm still not taking medication. I find the stranger easier to manage when I throw myself into my work. I never thought mental health could be a beautiful distraction. I find it exhilarating when providing care for the population I serve. I champion for their care. I champion for their rights. I champion for a better way of life for them. I find teaching others about mental illness will help change the stigma others have. I always tell people, "They are the same as you and I, they just think differently." And even though how I deal with the stranger is very unconventional, it's what works for me. My struggle continues, but I look forward to life. Every day I wake up is a blessing for me and someone else.

Who Gets Sad Looking at Butterflies?

Adonicca MeChelle

I am educated, driven, and successful. I wish I could tell you that those characteristics kept me from experiencing mental health challenges, but unfortunately, that is just not how it works. I am educated, driven, and successful—and I live with anxiety and chronic depression. It's a funny thing—how people can know you well and never grow suspicious of the ailments that silently plague you. The depression is episodic; however, its marriage to anxiety has ushered me to many of the lowest moments in my life. These moments have been confusing and scary. These moments also intersect with several traumatic experiences.

People like for stories to be linear, a straight line from beginning to end. Trauma prevents people like me from having the ability to do this. I'm not sure which came first: the trauma or the mental health obstacles. I'm not sure if it matters. What I know is that, as a result of the trauma I have sustained, I have few specific memories of my childhood.

I grew up in a two-parent household, which was growing more and more uncommon in that time, and we had a decent home. Yet most of my memories as a kid are dark, painful, confusing, and bonded with trauma. From an early age, I prided myself on being bright and independent. The grown-ups in my life would probably refer to me as strong-willed, and I suppose in a way that would be accurate. But while I would not describe myself as defiant, I was determined. My determination often manifested in unhealthy ways and showed up as a need for approval, validation, and over-functioning. I now know to call this anxiety, and while I am not sure the exact moment it appeared in my life, I know the things that contributed to it.

It may seem like an oversimplification, but as a youth, I never thought I was pretty. I was always taller than the other kids, I was chunky, and I never quite felt like I fit in socially because I was always evaluating whether the slightest movements I made were the right ones. I always felt that if I couldn't be pretty, I could be anything else. If I couldn't be pretty, I could be *everything* else.

Manifestation/Caterpillar

The first time I felt like I wanted to die, I was thirteen. I was in charge of my younger brother, his friend, and my younger cousin who was five years old. My dad was napping because he often worked overnight. My mom was out of town with a couple of her girlfriends. Earlier that day, my dad had made a seven-layer chocolate cake. He told us not to touch it, he was so excited about it. My five-year-old cousin had recently learned to pour, and she wanted to show me how she could pour a glass of orange juice. Since I was in charge, I allowed it. My leg was in a brace from a sports injury, so I merely supervised. She was beaming with pride as she poured, but lost her grip on the bottle and spilled orange juice everywhere—all over my dad's cake.

We could clean the kitchen floor to make sure it wasn't sticky, and we could wipe down the countertop. What we couldn't do was hide the fact that we ruined something that my dad was so proud of. Since I was the oldest and since I was in charge, I was the one who got punished. Whether or not the punishment fit the crime is moot at this point in time; however, my response to the punishment was something I had never experienced. I went upstairs and locked myself in the bathroom. I paced the floor, ashamed that I had let my dad down and couldn't handle being in charge for a few short hours. I couldn't breathe. Tears in my eyes, I ran the water in the bathroom sink and covered my mouth. I wanted to scream, but I was too embarrassed to be heard. I felt lost and confused and stupid and not good enough. I may have been having my first anxiety attack. In that moment, I wished I were not alive.

Treatment/Chrysalis

When I was a kid, I was sick a lot. I often called my mom from school to pick me up. I was clumsy, so sometimes it was an injury or nosebleed. Then there were less visible things that I left school for, like stomach aches, frequent migraines, and unbearably painful menstruation. One day, one of the doctors had a chat with my mother about the possibility of my needing a light antidepressant. I was in junior high, and the doctor was a Black female. She recognized something that no one in my life had ever acknowledged. I felt a tiny sliver of hope when she introduced the idea that a medication may help to get me on track; however, my mom was offended by the idea that I could be depressed. We never revisited the possibility again.

I continued dealing with the fusion of depression and anxiety through my journey to adulthood. In college, I sought my own solutions and tried my best to treat my own traumas. Then, when I was in my mid-twenties, I hit an unprecedented low. The circumstances leading to this spiral are not as important as the severity of this episode and how scary the reality was. I had challenges with migraines daily, which were seemingly unrelated to stress, and I stopped going to my job. I called out for days in a row and spent that time crying alone. I stopped eating regularly, and I had nightmares every night. I had people who loved me, but I'm not sure I felt supported or understood. I shrunk into myself.

One of these days, I had an appointment to see my neurologist about my migraines. My doctor was fond of me and often told me that I reminded him of his daughter. While waiting for my appointment, my anxiety sent me into a frenzy and I felt like I was falling apart. I left, and took a drive to clear my head. My head couldn't be cleared. Instead, I cried while driving. I couldn't breathe. I felt worthless for one reason or another, and the world was spinning out of control. In this moment, while I was driving, I envisioned myself crashing. Instead, I made it home and locked myself in my bedroom. I cried. I covered my face, and I wanted to scream, much like I did that time when I was thirteen.

At the next appointment, while waiting on my doctor, I wrote him a short, frantic note in panicked handwriting:

Please help me. I don't know what to do. I don't know what's wrong with me. I feel afraid that I might hurt myself. I do not know why. I am doing the best I can. I can't handle this. I don't know what I'm doing. My migraines are really bad, and I also feel like I do not want to live. I do not have a best friend and I do not think I can tell anyone in my family. I need help and you are the only person I feel like I can talk to. I wrote this note because I was afraid that I would change my mind about asking for help. I need help. Please help me.

I sat in the dim waiting room waiting to be seen, and I was barely holding it together. I held my breath so that I would not burst into tears. I rocked back and forth, staring blankly at the wall across from me. When my doctor came out to get me, I stood up, tears flowing from my eyes as I walked behind him to the exam room. I handed him the note, which was the first bravest thing I did that day.

My doctor connected me with an office that had both a psychiatrist and a counselor. They did not have appointments until a few hours later, and I didn't want to be alone. My neurologist allowed me to stay comfortably in his office until it was time for me to see them.

Some hours later, feeling completely despondent and like I was ready to break, I went to the psychiatrist's office. I walked in, noting the all-white décor with silver accents. There was a sign on the desk that said the staff were on break and to sit in the waiting room. I sat, observing how clean and quiet the waiting room was. The next part sounds silly, but "(Sittin' On) The Dock of The Bay" by Otis Redding was playing, and I started to cry, thinking that I must have been dead because I had always heard that the song was about wanting to die.

Eventually, a nurse escorted me to the psychiatrist's office, and I waited in silence. In front of me was a painting of four butterflies and tree branches against a Carolina blue sky. There were three brownish-orange butterflies in the center of the painting and one butterfly, all alone, off to the right. As I looked at the butterfly to the right, my face became flushed and I held my breath in an effort to keep my tears at bay. *Why was the butterfly to the right all alone?* That was the depression. My next immediate thought was to criticize myself. I felt ashamed. *Who gets sad looking at butterflies?* That was the anxiety. I felt alone, just like the butterfly on the right.

The second bravest thing I did that day was also the scariest decision I have ever made: I agreed to be hospitalized for treatment.

Emergence/Butterfly

Hospitalization is one of the scariest experiences I have ever had—and one of the most important. After the hospitalization,

I continued with therapy and medication to treat the anxiety and depression. For a while, I felt my symptoms were alleviated, yet I did not quite feel like I was progressing. Instead, I was in less pain, having less intense thoughts, and finding it difficult to show enthusiasm. While I enjoyed having a once-a-week outlet in my therapist, I found it difficult to connect with her, which made me feel disappointed in myself. After a year or so, I decided to continue my medication but end therapy. I continued to quietly struggle with adjusting to the world around me, cocooned in being educated, driven, and successful.

I continued seeking therapists, but ultimately none fit. I pushed myself to be intelligent and determined, and I excelled in my career much like I excelled as a youth in academia. It was not until years later, after a long-term abusive relationship ended, that I found a therapist who fit me. I was challenged to emerge from my cocoon and untangle the experiences that had contributed to the anxiety and the depression.

This new chapter in life could only be supported by dedicating my energy and hard work to myself. The most important things that I have learned on this journey are to:

1. Call it out.

When the feelings creep in, acknowledge it to the best extent possible. Name it if you can. Certainly, this depends on the severity of the episode and how your mental health is managed. I have found this to be helpful with episodes, but this may not be helpful in a crisis.

2. Ask for help.

Suffering alone is not necessary. I felt alone and without friends. I was afraid to tell my family my feelings and was unsure of where to turn. Find one person—just one—who you can trust to support you in finding help in the event of an emergency. If this person is close to you, discuss a plan for recurring episodes.

3. Position yourself to receive the help that fits you.

I have learned that the most important part that comes after asking for help is being in a position to receive the help. Finding a therapist is among my least favorite things, next to dates and job interviews. These three things share a common risk: not knowing how well you will connect and whether or not the option is the right option for you. It can be frustrating and discouraging.

4. Draw boundaries.

In asking for help, you may feel obligated to share more of yourself than what feels safe or necessary. Admittedly, boundary setting has been a struggle and cost me a lot of peace. On my journey, I have learned that there is power in vocalizing boundaries with those who you trust to support you. This does not mean to hide your suffering or any harmful thoughts; rather, it means that you do not owe everybody access to your trauma—especially people who are not mental health professionals.

5. Go to therapy consistently; it is active work.

The work that I have done (and continue to do) in therapy is important, active work. This work requires the proper support to continue adjusting to the outside world. As with developing any healthy habit, consistency yields results.

I wish I could say that I do not still struggle with the pressure of anxiety or the fear that depression will creep up on me. For a while, I wondered if I would regress to the scary, low moments that depression has shown me. I feel, however, that the likelihood is lower because of the treatment that I continue to receive. I am educated, driven, and successful—and I live with anxiety and episodic depression. I am a leader, I am a public servant, and I am actively engaged in therapy.

I am pretty, and I can be anything else.

I am pretty, and I can be *everything* else.

Even a butterfly.

On the Other Side of FOG

Jacinth McAllister

I am love. I am purpose. I was made with divine intention.

—Rebekah Borucki

I have always disliked fog, especially driving through it because your vision is limited, leaving you fearful of what might jump out in front of your vehicle. You have to reduce your speed, find the correct light setting (low beams or fog lights), and use your hazard lights, allowing people to label you as one of "those drivers." Fog causes you to take longer to get to your destination.

As much as I dislike fog, it managed to hang around in my life for sixteen long years. The fog I am referencing is not the fog I mentioned driving through, but fear, obligation, and guilt (FOG).

August 30, 2002, was the day I lost one of the most important and influential people in my life, my daddy, Bishop Theodore McAllister Jr. He was a girl dad, and I was a daddy's girl! He was not just my daddy, but my pastor, my friend, my confidant, and my teacher of many things. He was my little piece of heaven on Earth.

When I left for work that morning, I had no clue it would be the last time I saw my father alive. The last few months had been difficult for him, but I thought he would pull through like he always did. Little did I know, he was tired of pulling.

I was at work for less than an hour when I got the call that there was an emergency at home and that someone was on the way to pick me up. When I arrived home, I was met by police officers and CCBI crime scene investigators who had roped our yard off with crime scene tape. Family and friends looked on from across the street. A detective approached, verified my identity and relation, and escorted me into the house to join my family.

"Where is my daddy?" I asked.

Everyone's attention turned to me, but no one said a word. My mother mouthed to the detective, "She doesn't know."

"Know what?"

"I'm sorry, ma'am, but there has been an accident and your father is dead."

"Accident?"

The detective's face and disposition softened, and in the sincerest tone, he responded, "I'm sorry, ma'am, it was suicide."

In that life-changing moment, my world shattered. The words "daddy," "dead," and "suicide" swam around in my head aimlessly as I tried to process what had just been told to me. My daddy was lying lifeless in our family den, behind crime scene tape, with strangers hovering around his body, a single gunshot wound to his chest.

That night, I went to bed, and FOG began its descent over my life. I was fearful of living life without my daddy. I felt obligated to look strong so no one would know the depth of my grief and guilt. I was the last person to see him alive and was not able to recognize that he was on the brink.

After we buried Daddy and things settled down, I still had questions. Outside of the spiritual realm, there seemed to be nowhere to turn. I took on two of the cliché pieces of advice I received: "you just need to get back into a routine, baby" and "just try to shift your focus." I suppressed every question and emotion I had about my daddy's suicide. I turned on my high beams and went on a dangerously emotional and unhealthy drive in FOG land from the age of nineteen through most of my adult life.

My daddy's death shook the community, and rumors and speculation swirled about the Black preacher who killed himself. I was constantly on the defense to protect my father's legacy, ready to attack anyone who uttered disdain against his name. While fighting people and my emotions, FOG was pulling me deeper and deeper into grief. While fearful of peoples' judgments and opinions, I felt even more obligated to look and be strong.

I resolved to remain a pillar of strength for my family while guilt was now joined by shame. Externally I appeared strong, but internally I was hurting, weak, angry, despondent, and broken. I was a nineteen-year-old struggling to try and balance motherhood, work, school, and home life. I knew I needed help but did not know where to turn; therefore, I accepted these struggles as life for me and drove faster in my FOG.

This drive through FOG began to get difficult. While missing my daddy, I started looking for love in all the wrong places. I found myself in recurring verbally abusive and emotionally unhealthy relationships. These relationships left me more broken with even lower self-esteem. With these abandonment issues, codependency and attachment anxiety surfaced in my life.

I allowed others to project their insecurities and fears onto me. I was afraid to vocally defend myself out of fear of being called crazy. I was an obligor and put others' needs before my own, which left me emotionally depleted. The feeling of guilt for "rocking the boat" kept me in toxic situations longer than I should have been.

I finally tore myself away from toxic relationship cycles and spent a few years alone. During this time, I grew closer to God by joining a biblically based church, focused on my physical health, and focused more time and energy on my teenage son. My devotion and prayer life were consistent, and I was in a better place physically, mentally, and spiritually. The FOG that had covered my life for the past fourteen years seemed to shift—a little bit.

By this time, I was a thirty-three-year-old single mother ready to love and be loved. I found myself back in a relationship with a familiar person and felt certain we would live happily ever after. I felt stronger mentally, emotionally, and spiritually. I promised myself things would be different. No longer would I suppress hurt or pain; I would speak up for myself.

The honeymoon phase, or what I now know as the gas-lighting phase, of my second-time-around relationship lasted for a few months, and things were great. I was quickly reminded that as long as I did not "rock the boat," things would remain great. When I did speak up for myself, it was met with passive aggressive behavior in the form of the silent treatment for days. He involved my close friends and relatives (triangulation) in our disagreements in an attempt to pit them against me. The silent treatments were initially far and few between, but then began an unbearable progression. My feelings were dismissed by statements such as, "I don't know why you feel that way" or "You are crazy for feeling that way." Changing my recount of what I knew to be true was his mission.

Before I knew it, confusion, guilt, and shame had crept in, and I resumed suppressing my pain and feelings. I was afraid to leave the relationship because I did not want to "wake up" from my "happily ever after dream." I was caught up in the FOG: (fear) of choosing my own mental and emotional well-being, (obligation) to accept the blame, and (guilt) to believe that I was the cause for his negative behavior.

I cried and prayed and asked God to heal my relationship. God kept showing me images of my healed self getting out of the relationship with the use of a third party. Thinking I knew better than God, I ignored the signs and continued on my dangerous drive through the FOG. It got so bad I could not see left or right, forward or backward. At that moment, I was convinced that I needed professional counseling.

I took responsibility for my healing. I researched counselors and psychologists for three weeks, and after several dials and hang-ups, I successfully scheduled an appointment. My first appointment went something like this: I walked in, sat on the couch, and blurted out, "My name is Jacinth McAllister, I have a whole bunch of suppressed trauma, my daddy committed suicide sixteen years ago, I'm in a relationship with this man, and everything is my fault so I need you to fix me. Can you do it?" I could not believe I said all of this, seemingly, in one breath.

My counselor was unfazed by my spill and gathered more information. We talked seamlessly for my allotted time. It felt so good to release some of what I had been holding onto for years, so once the session was over, I scheduled my next appointment.

I went to counseling in secret for over a month, partly because I was embarrassed but mainly because I wanted to do something for me! As I became equipped with the proper tools for healing and communication, my once FOG-filled life seemed to become a little clearer. In that clarity was a harsh reality I was not ready to face.

I left counseling one day so excited that I decided to tell my boyfriend about it. He immediately accused me of being sneaky and secretive and ensued the silent treatment. This time, I was not having it. My high beams were on and ready to see me through this FOG. Instead of trying to reason with him verbally, I decided to use one of my newly learned tools: writing. In my written communication, I explained my feelings, the place I had progressed to, and my hope for our future. That letter ultimately caused our relationship to end, and I could now add healing from an emotionally unhealthy relationship and broken heart to the counseling list.

FOG had now attached itself to my old relationship. I was fearful of what people would think of me for breaking up my externally "perfect" relationship. I felt obligated to remain in that relationship because things were supposed to work out this time. I carried guilt, thinking that had I not written that letter, we would still be together.

In that moment of reckoning with the letter, I learned to always stand in my truth, even if I have to stand alone. It also taught me to take accountability for my part in my relationships and delayed self-healing. The emotional trauma in the relationship was hurting me. I accepted that it was unhealthy to deal with a person who accepted minimum accountability and repeated behavior. There is truth in the saying, "Doing the same old thing yields the same old results."

I continued counseling, and we dug into my childhood, my relationship with each parent, sibling relationships, sexual abuse, and friendships. At times, it was too much to bear! I walked out in the middle of sessions and even canceled appointments. A few times, I reasoned that I was healed, but my commitment to my emotional healing was more important and I resumed my sessions.

What I learned in this time was that I had to face the deepest and darkest truths for effective healing. I wrote my way through seven journals during my sixteen-month mental wellness treatment plan. I recounted the highs and lows of every single day of my healing. Some entries were fifteen pages long, while others were barely half a page. There were days I would sit on my living room floor and cry and pray until my tear ducts were dry and my voice was barely a whisper. I thought God had led me on this journey only to forget me. I thought I was going to run out of tears and sanity before I got through this treatment plan.

Just as I was entering eye movement desensitization and reprocessing (EMDR) to replace negative thoughts with positive ones, my pastor started a preaching series entitled "I Quit." Every sermon in that series somehow aligned with my counseling sessions. That is when I knew God had not left me and that I was on the way to where I needed to be spiritually and emotionally.

The cloud of FOG—fear, obligation, and guilt—that once covered my life was now being replaced with a new FOG— fearlessness, opportunity, and grace. I was now fearless to live my life and embrace every opportunity in an emotionally healthy way. Counseling has helped me manage anxiety and emotions, improve the way I communicate, and improve my interpersonal skills. It has helped me forgive myself and my abusers. I am able to replace negative emotions with positive ones. My self-esteem allows me to practice self-acceptance, which helps me to overcome codependency and release my feelings of guilt. By living an emotionally healthy life, I honor my daddy's legacy daily.

The biggest keys to achieving and maintaining my healing are consistency, transparency, and accountability. Everything takes work, and it's imperative that it's honest work. I invested in myself for the first time, and I hope you will too! You will love the results, I promise!

The journey to achieving mental, emotional, and psychological freedom is a tough one, but you owe it to yourself. Every moment of discomfort, every tear you will shed, every growing pain, will be worth it. I pray that if FOG is in your life that you will stay the course in healing:

- Love and trust yourself.
- Do not be ashamed to seek help.
- Find the right counselor.
- Surround yourself with supportive people.
- When it gets tough, let the tough get going.
- No pain, no gain!
- Never let your healing be contingent upon someone else.
- Lean on your faith.
- Have a devoted devotional life-study: God's Word, prayer, and meditation

Be steadfast and unmovable because on the other side is your healthy, transformed self waiting to welcome you!

Bipolar Disorder Caught Me by Surprise

Doris Beasley Haynes-Mullings

Going through life, I was on top of the world, always trusting, always full of simplicity and humility, content with whatever state I found myself in. I was a devout Christian and rejoiced greatly in the Lord, with my mind being renewed by the washing of the Word. I could relate to Paul when he said, "I am not saying this because I am in need, for I have learned to be content whatever the circumstances. I know what it is to be in need, and I know what it is to have plenty. I have learned the secret of being content in any and every situation, whether well fed or hungry, whether living in plenty or want. I can do all this through him who gives me strength" (Philippians 4:11-13 NIV).

As the saying goes, I was "riding high on life," enjoying my walk with Jesus Christ. I had a good job, I was driving a new car, I had bought a four-family rental property house. I had even gotten married for a second time. We had purchased a three-bedroom house with a beautiful wooden staircase leading upstairs to the bedrooms, a loft that we used for our office and extra sleeping space, a furnished finished basement, a living room with a fireplace, a formal dining room, and a full kitchen. The house also had a two-car garage.

My "riding high" here alludes to both elevated and elated status. I had attended New Jersey Evangelical Bible Institute and obtained a bachelor's degree in Christian Education/ Theology. I was successful, at least in the eyes of public opinion. I thought I was beginning to discover who I was and what my purpose was in life—and then it happened: my first bipolar/manic episode.

I had no idea what was going on in my mind, body, or soul. I had never had such feelings come over me. Everything I wanted the world to be was now coming true. There was positivity in almost everything, and I would see sunshine even when there were clouds in the sky. At first, I was waiting to wake up because it seemed surreal. As the days passed, things became what I thought was clear. In this state, there was absolutely no fear. I enjoyed the manic feelings—like I was on top of the world. I had an abundance of energy, and I was more creative than ever, more friendly, more talkative. I loved this new life, not knowing it was something called mania. I felt like I was living my best life.

Mania had me speeding without taking any pills. The manic behavior made sense later, after learning the same chemicals that are released in the brain from amphetamines may be released in the manic phase. My manic side effects were extreme happiness, restlessness, and increased activity. The mania disorder led to impulsive spending sprees like purchasing houses. I once purchased a church. I was starting businesses, but it was always to help others.

One day, it felt like I had fallen off the edge of a cloud and no one was there to catch me—not even Earth herself. It has been said, "What goes up must come down," and down was intense depression and despair.

I suffer from bipolar I disorder, which is the most serious form of bipolar disorder. In the beginning of my experiences with bipolar disorder, I simply could not realize what was going on. It was extremely confusing, to say the least. When I was in the "down state" (depression), my peace and happiness were gone, and I struggled to remember that God promised to always be with His people. He promised never to leave nor forsake me. There was a feeling that I had taken God's favor for granted, and it had landed me in this state. Although I was a believer in Jesus Christ and had over eighteen years of spiritual and emotional stability, something had changed, and it seemed out of my control. I found it difficult to pray, and fear had taken over my faith.

The "high state" is what I experienced before the lows. After going to therapy sessions, both individual and group, I found out this is how it affects some bipolar people's lives. I can now better recognize the symptoms of bipolar disorder, particularly when it comes to mania. These are signs I exhibit when in a manic state:

Extremely high levels of energy. I would wake up at 4:30 a.m. and go to the gym, swim for one solid hour, and wonder why others were taking breaks. I remember thinking to myself, these people are out of shape. After finishing my swim, I would shower, pamper myself a bit, blow-dry my hair (which was long at this time), style it, and get dressed and then drive to work to arrive by 7:30 a.m.

Fast-talking. Normally, I have a tendency to speak fast, but in this state, I would speak so fast that others could not understand what I was saying. I also would not give others a chance to speak. I knew everything and had all the answers.

Little need to sleep. In this state, I would maybe sleep three to four hours.

Easily distracted. I started several projects but was easily distracted and didn't complete any of them. Exhilaration filled me as I raced around working. It was as if the more work I created, the better I felt.

After months of energy and excitement, I would fall into a deep state of depression. I would become very weak and unconcerned. I would sometimes have zero interest from day to day, which brought a feeling of hoping I would die in my sleep. I went from needing only three to four hours of sleep to staying in bed all the time and sleeping a lot, barely eating due to a loss of appetite, going from a high level of self-esteem to feeling worthless, and having suicide ideations. I have had sad and crippling times, physically and mentally, during my twenty-four years with bipolar disorder.

My very first experience with the depression state happened on a Thursday, July 11, 1996. I began to sink into an uncharacteristic period of anxiety and, later, depression. I was overwhelmed with dark thoughts. I struggled to counteract the despair with the Word of God and with the help of the Holy Spirit. I never stopped praying, although God seemed so far from me.

My original feelings were confusion and denial. I could not accept that I was ill and needed medical attention. The thought of going to a doctor brought on more anxiety, as I did not believe in therapy. In my ancestry, family members cared more about what people would say if you needed psychiatric intervention. It would be better if I had cancer or a brain tumor. The prevailing attitude in Black communities is that Black people are strong, and they should just keep on climbing "Jacob's Ladder." It was believed that Black people have too many other problems to get depressed. If I had a dime for every time someone said "she is just lazy and needs to snap out of it," I would be rich. People all around were asking, "How could this happen to her? She is a strong Christian woman."

I did not want to go for a psychiatric evaluation when my sister Christine suggested it. I had visions of the hospital staff wearing white jackets, patients with straitjackets, empty padded cells, scenes from a movie I had seen, called *One Flew over the Cuckoo's Nest*. I feared going to see anyone who I felt could read my mind and had the power to put me in a mental ward. All of these feelings and visions stemmed from fear. To help me, the psychiatrist told me to remember the acronym FEAR:

> **F**alse
>
> **E**vidence
>
> **A**ppearing
>
> **R**eal

I still hold fast to this acronym with hopes that it can help someone else. And, speaking as a Christian for forty-five years, Christians are not exempt from any type of diseases; be not deceived. However, our God is a divine healer. He left us the Holy Spirit. In the New Testament, Jesus healed "every disease and every sickness," as well as plagues in the areas He visited (Matthew 9:35, 10:1; Mark 3:10).

Experts do not know exactly why someone develops bipolar disorder, and there is no one factor that sparks it. From my experiences, it was from stress due to certain changes in my life. I had moved to a new area over an hour away from close friends and family, and I found out my now ex-husband was molesting my daughter. This was a major contributing factor and was highly upsetting. I had a child less than two years old with no support system nearby. I was also dealing with the death of my brother Levi, who departed at the age of forty-five.

It is unclear specifically how, but genes can also play a large role, and bipolar disorder runs in my family. I believe my father and mother were chemically imbalanced but never diagnosed. I have three brothers and a sister who were diagnosed with some type of mental illness.

Living with bipolar disorder is not easy for me, and I realize it also makes life extremely hard for the people around me. The manic phase of this disease is exhilarating when experiencing it, but not so much for your friends and family. When people are in the manic stage of bipolar, it feels like they can do anything, which often causes them to engage in risky behaviors—impulsively quitting their jobs, spending their savings, and making other types of sweeping life changes—which can hurt themselves or loved ones. Therapy has been beneficial in helping me see the effects I have on others and knowing that effect helps me make sure I take my medications and continue therapy.

Since 1989, I have had an exceptionally good friend in New Jersey who is like my sister. She has been there for me since my first bipolar episode. It can be difficult for me in the manic phase to realize my behavior has changed because I always express great joy and happiness. However, I have people in my circle that know it is important to be aware of the signs and get help for me if necessary. If a person with bipolar disorder stops taking their medicine, that is one reason to call the doctor or urge them to do so; although if I am manic, I literally hate to be asked if I am taking my medication.

While going through a bipolar episode, I sometimes felt like I was a burden. To that end, when my family would ask me to go out, I would say no, all the time contemplating how to end this life. Do not be ashamed of the illness; there is not something we did to develop bipolar disorder. I have taken my son, my daughter, and other family members to my doctor's appointments to ask questions or give their perspectives on how I am doing. My younger sister Naomi has always been there to listen, without judgment. The stigmas attached to mental illnesses continue to be evident. But you are not crazy. Check out PsychCentral.com, where you can find informative bipolar information and quizzes. But please note that it is not for anyone who is looking to be diagnosed.

Here are my recommendations for anyone who suffers from a bipolar disorder:

1. Know that you are not alone.

2. Seek professional help. Bipolar disorder is a lifelong condition that creates unusual mood changes that can vary in length and severity.

3. Have no fear of being hospitalized.

4. Comply with what is recommended by your health team.

5. Form a support group and share with them to develop a better understanding of and response to bipolar episodes and have plans. If people in my support group do not hear from me over three to four days, they should check in on me and see if everything seems to be normal; if not, they will notify others in the group. When I was in a bipolar state, I wanted no one around me, and this is the last thing a person in a low phase of bipolar needs.

6. Do not make your support group too large. My support group consists of six people, including someone who suffers from bipolar disorder.

7. Do not look for a quick fix.

8. Do not compare yourself with other people who have bipolar disorder.

9. Stay hopeful! Bipolar disorder is a disease that can be managed with medication, therapy, and a support team. Check for local group meetings.

10. Local group therapy is a source of strength and hope, which is important for recovery, especially because it can take a long time.

Bipolar disorder is like many other types of illnesses that can be manageable with medication and therapy. I praise God my experiences with bipolar disorder are manageable today and I have not had an episode in over ten years. Although I have ups and downs, I have been able to live a productive life with fun, meaning, and connection. To anyone who has been diagnosed or may be diagnosed during this journey called life, although it may seem like life might as well be over, it is not. We can still live and enjoy our best life.

Why Not Me?

Jennifer Norman

Post-traumatic stress disorder (PTSD) is a diagnosis the military gave me. Nowadays, the term feels all too synonymous with military personnel. However, my story does not involve explosions or wartime as seen on television, and while I now know PTSD is a diagnosis given beyond war, I was someone who truly allowed myself to believe it was as shown in movies and news. My perception of PTSD was that of the military returning home from war with visible wounds.

While my story with my first experience with mental health starts in the military, I think it is important to highlight my life before my diagnosis. I grew up in Kenly, North Carolina, with working-class parents. My childhood was unremarkably normal in the sense of having two loving parents, a sister, and a healthy childhood experience. I left high school and attended a historically Black college/university (HBCU). I went to an HBCU because I wanted to be around other Black people. I loved college. I partied 90 percent of the time, leaving little room for schoolwork. I realized I loved college too much and needed to settle into adulthood, so I dropped out of college and joined the Marine Corp. The Marine Corp was not my first option between the military branches, but I felt it was a way to prove how strong I am as a woman.

When I joined the Marines, I moved to California, where I got married and had my oldest daughter. Next, I moved to

Hawaii, where I had my youngest daughter. Then I moved to Camp Lejeune, North Carolina. My husband was in the field, which meant he was always gone; he never missed a holiday, but he was gone every other day. By being active duty myself, I did not connect well with any of the other military spouses, and there were few women in the military who shared similarities.

Camp Lejeune is where I was stalked for about six months. Everyone I told kept thinking I was "crazy," and no one believed me. Strange things were happening: my keys went missing from my house more than once, I felt someone was looking in my windows, I found a footstep on my daughter's tricycle, and one evening, my neighbor came over and said the letters I was sending to my husband ended up in her backyard. I know I had placed each letter in the mail to be delivered to my husband. Being an individual from the South, I did not use the dead bolt because I felt safe; everyone assumed I had just misplaced my keys. Everyone came up with a reason for why these things were happening to me, and I let them make me believe their reasoning because I didn't want people saying I had lost my mind. However, I knew things were not adding up.

When it finally came to a head, my husband was gone. I was raped. In my home, while my children were asleep, someone took a piece of me, disrupting my sense of security. I was violated—more than violated. Someone took something from me that I have never been able to get back: the feeling of safety. After this occurred, my sense of stability and safety continued to topple, worsening from the remarks of others, the lack of support from my spouse, and worst of all, the accusatory actions of the Marines. Somehow this became my fault.

Was this the first time I dealt with a man feeling empowered through his attempt to use force against me? No. The Marine Corp recruiter "hemmed me up" in his office. He decided he was going to make me come over to the "Black side." It was a struggle, but I got out! That time, I was able to escape, but did I tell anyone? No.

After the rape, the military moved me into another house. Still, I felt unsafe. Our family then transferred to Japan on military orders, and my life began to rapidly come apart, strand by strand. While in Japan, my husband and I divorced, which was horrible. Divorce itself is ugly enough, but it becomes toxic when others have trauma to use against you. My ex-husband blamed me for not getting help. He did not want to get divorced, so he made the military believe that my lack of therapy was the sole reason for us to remain married. The Marine Corp wanted me to go to therapy, so I went, but it did not work for me. The Marine Corp placed everyone, from addicts to suicidal individuals, in a group therapy setting. How can I tell my story in a setting that does not fit my needs? Our stories and needs were far too different.

In Japan, it felt as if everyone in my command believed my ex-husband over me, labeled me as weak, and attempted to take away my power of decision. Everyone thought they knew what was best for me. The Marine Corp denied our divorce. On top of that, I was paranoid once again because I felt like the things that happened before the rape were still occurring. People did not believe me, and my rapist was still not caught. Even miles away, my rapist still held onto control. My money was missing, and I knew my husband was involved. I knew at that moment, the marriage was over; I had reached my breaking point.

Eventually the police in North Carolina found my rapist. They found him because he raped multiple other women. I did not go to the court date. He accepted a plea deal and admitted to his stalking, which proved I was not "crazy." The military finally left me alone and no longer pushed therapy. Unfortunately, I was given orders back to Jacksonville, North Carolina. I was diagnosed with PTSD several years after my return. I refused to seek any treatment in the military due to their actions and their refusal to believe me.

Despite the arrest of my rapist, the rape continued to take too much from me. I stopped sleeping that year, in 1991. I could not sleep immediately following my trauma, and I still cannot sleep at night. As a full-time working mother, I could not take medication to help aid in sleep and place these nighttime fears at bay; the dosage of medication needed for sleep would cause me to have trouble waking in the mornings. I would only fall asleep once my body eventually shut down. I would live off only two to three hours of sleep nightly.

The rape changed my life forever, and while he may be punished through the judicial system, my body and mind are forever punishing me. There are things I can no longer handle in my life, like smells, which trigger a feeling of un-easiness. I am scared more times than I am not, and I am always on alert. Despite feeling these things in everyday life, I push through because of my children. As my children are older, I realize I have more time for this fear and uneasiness to sit with me throughout my days and nights. I will never feel safe again.

I replay the rape often, and I find myself even question-ing if they have the right guy. Why would someone I had never seen in my life stalk me and disrupt my life in the most vile way possible? I always thought that maybe it was some-one that I said something "flip" to; maybe I cussed him out in the shopping line; maybe I said something to someone and he plotted payback on me. I did not know my attacker. Why did he select me? I never knew him, and I still do not know him. I look him up in the criminal system to see if he is still locked away. I have only seen his face in a mug shot. I can-not seem to connect my reality with this person. Trauma is life changing; PTSD is life changing. There are no answers. I cannot go back. I always ask, *God, why me?* I was doing the right thing, being the perfect wife, and doing my hardest to be the "perfect" person. I took care of my children, went to school—but none of that mattered.

Is there hope in trauma? As I get older, I realize there can by hope in the future. I have learned that taking time for ourselves is vital. We get married, sometimes it does not work out, and we try again. There is no perfect person, and we cannot make up for the horrors and the vile nature of another person. However, there is a lesson in my story. As I grow older, I ask, *why not me?* I was not paying attention to my surroundings. I had become complacent with my surroundings.

My PTSD is a lifelong battle. There are days when I manage well, and there are days when I realize I have not managed well, but I made it through. My diagnosis affects my mom, my dad, my current husband, and my children. My family worried for me and they continue to worry for me.

Along with my diagnosis, life is always up and down. In 2013, I lost my mom, and her death was more than I could bear. She was my best friend. I was inconsolable and completely lost. Every emotion I have ever held came out. After she died, I wanted to die too. While my mom was alive, I felt like she was my protector more so than my dad, even though he was my hero. Not until I sat and thought about telling my story did I realize why I took her death so hard. After my mom passed, for the first time in my life, I truly did not have to be strong for anyone but me—which means I am stuck with my own thoughts daily, with less structure and nonstop obligations. Now, add this loss to my ongoing battle with depression and anxiety.

After losing my mom, I began seeing a therapist and working on me. My rape and the loss of my mother took a lot out of me, but I hold onto my sanity for my children. While I am seeing a therapist, I do continue to struggle daily with my coping and mental health. Living with PTSD or a mental health diagnosis from trauma means sometimes healing never fully comes. Sometimes we live in a world in which we just survive for others. Our power now comes from being a supporter and healer for others because despite my peace in this world being taken, I know that I can provide safety for others, or at least a listening ear.

Therapy has never been the answer for me, but I do it because it is seen as the most logical step. However, talking about my life helps me and does provide me with a sense of purpose. Sharing my story gives me power. I have found that storytelling and supporting other individuals who have similar stories provide me with a more therapeutic path to healing.

There is nothing that will bring back my years of no sleep, my security, that moment of when something does not seem right and I cannot catch my breath. Nothing will bring that back. There are not enough drugs in the world to help me sleep and ease the memories. However, I am still here, and I wake up every morning and decide that I will continue to be present in life and find joy in life's small moments.

A Perfect Plan for Healing

Rosetta Marie Price

"For I know the plans I have for you," declares the Lord,
"plans to prosper you and not to harm you,
plans to give you hope and a future."

—Jeremiah 29:11 NIV

People who have experienced mental illness may have the same diagnosis, but each person's story is different. I was diagnosed with paranoid schizophrenia in my early thirties. I have had relapses, but presently, I have been without active symptoms and in recovery for over thirty years. For years, I wondered why this had happened to me. I wondered how I would rise above it all. I am eager to share my story as millions of people suffer from some sort of mental health illness.

Those who are experiencing psychological changes may wonder if God played a cruel joke. I really don't believe that. When I became mentally ill, peace in my life as I knew it was lost. At least, that was my initial understanding. As a devout believer in God going through mental health challenges, one of the most comforting things to happen to me was when strangers would tell me, "Jesus loves you." It warmed my heart, and I thanked them. I really believe, as Jeremiah 29:11 says, that God has a plan for us all.

Sharing my truth in my story of overcoming mental illness is a way of giving back to people who are misunderstood,

uplift those who experience stigma, and enlighten and educate society. I want to encourage the mentally ill, and I want
to change archaic beliefs of what mental illness looks like.
Many people believe that those with mental illnesses are violent and dangerous, when in fact, they are at risk of being
attacked or harmed themselves. Hopefully my story will offer
a fresh perspective on how mental illness is viewed.

I pray often that God will bless me continually with grace
and mercy, and that I may say the right things in every situation I encounter. I pray that I may help some lost soul as I
reveal God's plans and how they impacted my story of mental illness. Here is a prayer from a prayer book that gives me
inspiration:

Your changes touch my life with hope and mystery.
God of love and power, I come ready and eager to
experience your power working through me.
Amen.

(Prayer Moments with God, Publications International, Ltd. 2001)

When I was younger, I knew the difference between what
was real and what was imagined. So when I became ill in
my early thirties, I knew something was not right. I questioned what was going on with my strange feelings and tried
to seek help. I went to a psychiatrist I found in the yellow
pages. My mistake. He charged me fifty dollars for a thir-
ty-minute session, and I was asked to leave because he had
another client coming. He did not offer medical solutions,

relaxation techniques, or ways of getting help. I felt dismissed and let down. Fortunately, my story doesn't end with a life full of mental anguish and confusion. I found help, but there are countless individuals with no outlet or anywhere to turn. Most people with mental health issues are found living on the street or poorly functioning in our society.

My story is unique, so let me go back to my youth. All through school, I wanted to be involved in various social clubs. I wanted to be a cheerleader, so in the seventh grade, I tried out. To my surprise, I made the squad. Then, I competed in a high school pageant and was elected Miss Congeniality. I still have that award. I passed to the tenth grade and worked part-time after school at Slacks Boutique because I had a love for clothes and fashion. I was elected to be Miss Fashionette and received the best-dressed award in school.

When I graduated from twelfth grade, I did not want to go to college right away. I wanted to travel, so I did research on becoming an airline stewardess. I was able to land an interview for the airline, so I went to Dallas-Fort Worth, Texas, for training as a reservation sales agent. I performed that job for three years. After three years of working as a reservation specialist, I went to Pittsburg, Pennsylvania, for flight attendant training. I earned my wings after eight weeks of training. I stayed with the airline for three and a half years. The man I call my father, Mr. Jack Miller, was the pilot who flew with me on the BAC 1-11. He was the captain, and I flew as senior flight attendant.

I loved the airline, but the stress and demands of work seemed to be weighing me down, and my life seemed to fall apart. I began to worry about leaving my daughter, Angela, for days. I felt pressured, worried, and stressed out. I thought I could help myself by recalling facts I had learned when I took classes in psychology, but it didn't help me understand or explain what was wrong with me. I went to all the wrong people. I fell into a depression. Simple things seemed complicated. I became nervous and jumpy. I could not think straight or concentrate. Thoughts constantly raced through my head. I lost weight. I was not eating or sleeping. I was experiencing auditory hallucinations, and I was frightened. I confessed to another flight attendant that I could hear Angela crying from a distance, but I was on the airplane working. Angela was at home. I thought someone was harming my daughter. Now I know these were delusions (false beliefs) and paranoia. The people I thought I could confide in talked about me and laughed at me behind my back.

After experiencing the auditory hallucinations, I was sent to Crownsville Hospital. I stayed in the mental health ward for one month, and then I ended up in St. Elizabeth Hospital. At first, I refused medication and told the doctor if I kept hearing voices, I would kill myself. The staff eventually convinced me to take the medication to calm the racing thoughts in my mind. Now I know accepting the care given to me by the medical professionals at the hospital was the best thing I could have done. I slept for the first time in a long while and was able to get mental clarity.

After six months of counseling, medication, and prayer, I recovered from my initial diagnosis of paranoid schizophrenia. I felt a sense of renewal, so I enrolled in the University of the District of Columbia and received an associate's degree in criminology. Then, in my junior year of college, I had a relapse. The relapse occurred after I stopped taking my medicine. I did not realize that I had to take medicine for the rest of my life. This time, I listened to the doctor and started back on my medicine.

After taking a break from school to get well mentally, I reenrolled in college to finish my pursuit of a bachelor's degree in criminal justice. I was so excited to see my supports there, at my graduation: my daughter, Angela, and "my father," Jack Miller.

After receiving my undergraduate degree from the University of the District of Columbia, I did not feel content. I decided to pursue counseling at Prince George's Community College. I took courses there as a prerequisite for counseling. After graduating from PGCC, I went to Bowie State University. While I was in school, I gained weight from my medication, but I no longer cared. I understood the importance of taking my medication. I was my old healthy self. I was confident, I had a clear mind, and I had a good support system behind me.

While enrolled in graduate school, my professor hired me to work for the mobile crisis unit working up close and personal with individuals in mental health crises such as paranoia, delusions, and hallucinations. I worked full-time, and my supervisor helped me balance school and work. Between the help of my college professors at Bowie State University and my supervisor at mobile crisis, I accomplished my goal of graduating with a master's degree in counseling and obtaining a job in the mobile crisis unit. Once again, my professors, supervisors, family, and friends all became a part of my positive support system.

If you have a mental illness, a support system is your mental health lifeline on your road to recovery. I almost committed suicide because I did not understand the importance of having a positive, encouraging village of people around me. A support system is comprised of people who care about your well-being, can provide you with healthy coping skills, and can offer tools for reducing depression, anxiety, and stress. Support systems played a significant impact on my recovery and how I am today. There were and are many people who served and serve as comforters in my life. Jack Miller was a devout believer and man of God. He was a positive influence in my life and the key for my progress. My daughter, Angela, an intelligent, outgoing, and strong woman of faith, is another powerful supporter, who never denied me even through the rough times of my illness. If it were not for caring, supportive people, I would not have a story.

Mental illness is a malfunction of the brain that affects the way a person thinks, but I want you to know that you can recover. God will send people your way to help. You may think it is a coincidence or an accident, but it's not. Whatever you think, just know God said, "For I know the plans I have for you . . . plans to prosper you and not to harm you, plans to give you a hope and a future." I gained a lot of inspiration from God's words. Go get help, especially when you find people who want to help you, and take your medication if prescribed.

Now, I have a wonderful extended family. My daughter is married to the best husband and son-in-law a mother can ask for, and his mother is warm and caring. My two grandchildren are smart, fun, energetic, and eager to learn. Angela's father and his wife never exclude me from family gatherings, celebrations, and visitations to their home. We continue to share fond memories to this very day. My friends have been supportive by providing a listening ear, grabbing a bite to eat, or joining me on a shopping excursion or trip to the movies. Jack Miller made sure I furthered my education.

I think back on all the people who ridiculed me because I suffered from a mental illness, and when I tried to commit suicide. Now, I say to those who are suffering from mental illness, don't let the taunting torment you. Don't let the ones who ridicule you cause you emotional pain or distress. For those who are mocked, let go and let God. God's revenge is mighty and swift. During the most trying times of my life, God didn't let me be harmed, nor did he let me die. I have hope and a future. I have been a professional counselor for twelve years, I have a master's degree, and I'm working on getting my license. I gained more than I lost, and so can you. Continue to be encouraged and work on eradicating the stigma of mental illness, especially among men and people of color. It is okay to seek help. It does not make you weak. In fact, it takes courage and insight to understand and seek help to become whole.

The Beauty of Finding Me in Spite of Me

Denise M. Simmons

In a perfect world, one size fits all; however, in the world that God designed just for me, that ideology is the furthest from the truth. For years, I thought God placed me in the "deal with it later" category because I couldn't possibly be plagued with mental health issues, too. I already had many other challenges to deal with that were the aftermath of my youth. In my late thirties, I was told I have mental health issues. This was way too intense for a small-town girl to hear when I was on the verge of making major changes in my life.

Born and raised in the northeast region of the United States, I was a little Black girl living in a predominately white suburban neighborhood. At that time, some folks would have said my family was an up-and-moving Black family who made it to the good side of the railroad tracks. On the contrary, I felt like life in suburbia with my family was not as glamorous as some may have thought it to be. My youth was filled with turmoil inside and outside of the home. I believed my family lived in a domestically challenged household, filled with bitter secrets, derogatory untruths, and constant chaos.

To add fuel to the fire, I was stricken with a physical handicap at birth that caused a range of reactions, from the awkward but inquisitive stares from curious small children to the most condemnatory actions from adults who did not have the decency to pretend my handicap was not a big deal. Perhaps God did not know what to do with me when I was in the incubation stage of my mother's womb. Perhaps His focus was elsewhere when my nine-pound body was brought into this life on Easter Sunday. Perhaps I was a punishment that resulted from the misbehaviors of someone else. Regardless of the reasons why I am here living this life with mental health issues, I have come to terms with my purpose in life—and God's purpose for me.

It was a long and discomforting process to understand my purpose. I did not have acceptance on "why me?" and preferred to command "why not them?" The truth of the matter is simple—because it is for you and not for them. What God has for me is for me, and no one else can change that. The book of Matthew, chapter 9 resonates with me because it demonstrates how Jesus engages with the people and answers the prayers of those who believe in His power to do so.

So here I was in my thirties—angry, frustrated, confused, and bewildered—looking for reasons to create chaos in my life. It took an uncomfortable conversation with my mother to acknowledge I had to be responsible for my mental health. At that moment, when I did not hear the response I was looking for in the conversation, I knew I needed to find a better way to help myself. There were so many reasons to find peace and harmony for my life, and I had to find another way to cope with my mental chaos. Thus, I scheduled an appointment with my doctor.

The day my doctor advised me that I have symptoms that are associated with mental health and depression was not a surprise to me. I had already believed I was depressed before getting the formal medical diagnosis and was prepared to accept medication to "fix me." I knew I wasn't happy all the time; however, I wasn't sad all the time either. For me, the glass was half full, and I never thought about hurting myself or doing anything that would cause me pain. The problem became obvious when I started thinking about how much I disliked some folks in my life and wanted them to experience the same depth of pain that I had held in my soul for decades. Now *that* is a problem.

The diagnosis from the doctor on that beautiful sunny day couldn't have come any sooner to stop me from having a complete mental breakdown.

"Hi, my name is Dee, and I suffer with depression."

I spoke these words as if I were in the Alcoholics Anonymous meetings I used to jitney my uncle to throughout the tristate area back in the early 1980s. I kept saying that phrase to myself the entire drive home from the doctor's office because I wanted to put a face to what I had been feeling all of these years: emptiness, hatred, anguish, pain, suffering, and acceptance that I possess the horrific disease some of my family members would refer to as being "crazy in the head." All of these sensations I felt for years were wrapped up into a medical diagnosis the doctor explained as "a slight case of depression associated with medical mental health conditions." The doctor advised the condition requires mental health therapy, a balanced diet, and medication. Medication! What? I have to take medication for my depression?

The process to manage my mental health condition with medication was a feat to say the least. What type of medication do I have to take? What dosage? It was a struggle for me to think about how I remain aware of the proper balance of mental health medications, minimize the consumption of the foods that stimulate a chemical imbalance, and maintain an active role in psychiatric therapy. The saga of mental health medication continues today.

Mental health medication management is not a bad thing; however, it can be if the mental health patient is unwilling to travel the journey to mental health awareness and understand the dynamics that go with the territory. Initially, my struggle to identify the best mental health remedy was overwhelming due to my limited knowledge on mental health awareness. I understood the proper mental medication had the potential to improve my mood swings. However, I was reluctant to take mental health medication because I had not accepted my mental health illness.

The answers to the whys are where the beauty of my story begins. When I finally accepted the fact I had mental health issues, I sought to get medication to help stabilize my mood swings. My initial exposure to mental health medication included various versions of antidepressants and mood stabilizers. I tried a few antidepressants, and they made me feel loopy, whereas the other antidepressants gave me no reactions. My experiences with mood stabilizers were not far from the experiences I had with the antidepressants. A few versions of the mood stabilizers worked for about six months to a year, and then the depression behaviors returned with a vengeance. This was the case for the next few years as I played mental health medication roulette in an effort to find the best medication to address my depression issues at that time. And just to think, the evolution of my mental health medication transformation was just beginning.

In my mid-forties, I realized so much time was wasted on trying to camouflage my truth to the world and not finding the correct medication that offered long-term relief. I had accepted I have a mental condition that needs medication, but I couldn't find the right medication to end the medical problem. But wait—my mood swings have increased significantly over the last few years, and my forties began with troubled waters. And now I have anxiety, too. *What?* Not only am I "crazy in the head," but I have a cognitive behavioral disorder? Are you kidding me? I had to accept yet another failure of mine and look for every opportunity in a situation that I found to be derogatory, pitiful, and downright unjust. Denial kicked in, and I became numb to my mental health condition. One month went by, another month went by, and finally, I said to myself, "Houston, we have a problem." It was time for me to make changes to feel better, look better, and produce better, for real this time.

I had to learn that what I had been hiding for years was no longer small enough to hide. I was no longer the tough, fearless woman who was determined to prove to the world that I was okay. I suffer with depression and anxiety, and I was not okay. Some of the things I learned during this process of finding myself were by default and others were by circumstance. I noticed that my relationship with God was broken and not genuine. Although I attended every Sunday service, I knew the words to every hymn sung at the early morning services; I knew that was Sister So-and-So and she was a gift from God; I knew when the pastor tapped the left side of the podium that he was getting ready to deliver a robust finale of the sermon. But I didn't know who I was and why I was replaying the thing about me that I wanted to push aside and act like it didn't exist. I had an out-of-body experience and did not recognize myself. I could no longer ignore my mental health symptoms, and I was forced to commit to mental health awareness to find a resolution for my condition.

I had a hole in my heart. A mental health madness dagger was hanging from my arteries because I was not intentional about my spiritual roots and had lost my way trying to make everyone believe I was alright. I wanted to be accepted as normal. I did not want to suffer with two mental health conditions that needed the attention of medication. The enemy wants us to think we can't, we aren't able to, and life is okay without; however, it is about the belief in God that He can do it. Won't He do it! Yes, He will, and I had to get on my knees and pray for deliverance from my evil, to deliver me from my pain of knowing I have a sickness that will remain in my presence until the end of my journey here on Earth. Accept that what God seeds He will flourish.

I tried to fix myself. I tried to correct my deficiency. But I couldn't fix it. My mood swings and low bouts with depression were present from the time I woke up in the morning to the time I went to sleep at night. There were environmental and emotional triggers that caused my mood swings to become more intense than nonthreatening environmental and emotional situations. I tried to run away, but my mental health condition was a sprinter and was everywhere I was.

When I prayed to God for help and He did not answer me how I wanted or when I wanted, I became angry, frustrated, disgusted, and absolutely appalled that God did not think I was important enough to be fixed. God did not take away the doubts in my mind. He did not remove the animosity I had for the person I am. The Holy Father did not eliminate the lack of confidence I had when I was asked to complete tasks or when asked for my assistance to help others. I was not eradicated from the anger I felt when I saw the person in the mirror who I felt gave me this horrific disease. I blamed and continue to blame myself for not being able to stabilize my mental health conditions and find a long-term resolution that provides positive performance outcomes.

It was a fight to identify the correct medication and proper mental health management, and the process continues. The human body changes day by day, hour by hour, and moment by moment. Therefore, it is important to recognize that what may have worked yesterday may not be the end-all-be-all today. The process to having a happy medium with mental health medication varies and is dependent on the physical capabilities and mental abilities at the time the medications are administered. However, what God has for you is for you, and He does not make mistakes with what He has for you.

I was blind because I didn't see my anger. I was blind to mental health awareness, blind to what the Lord had planned for me. I realize I was not as close to God as I thought I was. When I got the message to cry out the distress of the pain I felt, I cried out to God. This time I did not expect God to do the work to fix me. I was ready to do the work myself to fix me.

The Bible says in Matthew 9:27-29, "As Jesus went on from there, two blind men followed him, calling out, 'Have mercy on us, Son of David!' When he had gone indoors, the blind men came to him, and he asked them, 'Do you believe that I am able to do this?' 'Yes, Lord,' they replied. Then he touched their eyes and said, 'According to your faith let it be done to you'" (NIV). I cried out and asked the Lord to have mercy on my soul and help me. There are several references in the Bible that say to cry out to the Lord. In particular, Psalms has various references saying to cry out to God. I could not continue to do what I was doing without His help. I had to realize I could not do things like I did before. I had to allow the Lord to deliver me. Elijah cried out, Josiah cried out, and God responded to both of their individual needs. I cried out and followed the Lord into the space just like the blind men followed Him into the house.

I did not stand on the outside and expect Jesus to come to me. I cried out to Him and went after Him to get a resolution. I could no longer cry out and just stand there and wait for Him to reach out to me. I had to go into the valley of the unknown and fear no evil. I had to stop waiting. I did not want to be the same. I had questions that needed answers. I had to ask the Lord declarative statements and believe God wanted me to take responsibility and ownership of my mental health condition. I kept denying myself because of how I saw myself and not how God sees me. I had to stop looking at where I was and view the open horizon of where I am and where I seek to go. I was in my "now" and had to open my mind, my heart, and my spirit to accept my "new" way of living with mental health and the two conditions, depression and anxiety.

My story does not offer a perfect one-size-fits-all ending that all is well after many years of turmoil; that is not the case for me. One size does not fit all in my perfect world. I used to think, *am I a mistake?* I have recognized that there was not one way to address my mental health condition. I had to accept I was not born into this universe by mistake. I had to believe in myself and take the initiative to help myself become mentally healthy. Did I have to experience everything I did with mental health awareness and mental health medication management? Yes, I did! God created me to do great things in the midst of my challenges to manage my mental health conditions.

The plight to sustain the perfect match of mental health medication, a balanced diet, and consistent and productive psychiatric therapy remains a constant challenge in my life. However, the stigma that I suffered with accepting my mental health condition that requires medication is no longer a battle. The biblical references from Matthew 9:27-29 gave me the confirmation I needed that God never left me. He was always there for me, and I will continue to work on handling my mental health conditions with mental health medication management. To God be the glory.

And Then I Knew!

La Kia M. Smith

Proud mother of three young men, disabled Veteran, multiple sclerosis warrior of twenty-one years, third-generation native District of Columbian, matriarch of my siblings. These were the roles in life I easily accepted, the badges I wore with honor. A role that I didn't plan, nor did I easily accept, was someone who was diagnosed with a mental health condition.

While working toward earning my bachelor's degree, I was introduced to my mental illness. One day, I returned home from the hospital after getting a steroid treatment because of a multiple sclerosis exacerbation. I had some ambulatory issues that made it difficult for me to do everyday tasks, like walking or cleaning the house, in a normal amount of time. The previous night, it had taken me four hours to clean the kitchen.

While I was in my room, my middle son was in the kitchen making me a peanut butter and jelly sandwich. After my steroid treatment, I usually couldn't taste anything except peanut butter and jelly sandwiches. I walked into the kitchen, noticed three crumbs on the counter, and immediately, something in my head went off.

"Why are there so many crumbs on the counter?" I asked.

My son didn't react and continued to make my sandwich. At this moment it was like on television when a character has the angel and devil on her shoulders. The angel said, *Why are you upset about the three crumbs? He's making you the sand-wich.* The devil said, *Unh unh, it took you four hours to clean this kitchen.*

I started to feel the heat in my body rising. I felt myself getting angry, and it was the worst type of anger. I was so mad that he had these crumbs on the counter. In my head, I was telling myself, *Something is wrong because why are you angry about this? What's going on in your brain?*

Finally, I couldn't take it anymore, and I began screaming, "What the hell? You got my kitchen dirty! Why are there so many crumbs on the counter when it took me forever to clean this up?"

The entire time I was screaming at my ten-year-old, he continued to make my peanut butter and jelly sandwiches— not one, but multiple sandwiches—without skipping a beat. I continued to simultaneously rage and tell myself that I'm crazy and something is wrong with me. *This is not real.*

Next thing I knew, my son's two friends came out of his room because I was screaming at the top of my lungs.

"Ms. Kia, are you okay?"

Before I could respond, my son said, "She's fine. It's just the medicine."

I looked at him while he continued to make my sand-wiches and then ran away to my room. I had just acted like a maniac in front of all of these children, and my son was non-chalant about everything. Though this experience felt new to me, given my son's response, it was obviously not his initial experience with my mood swings and instability. There must have been other instances of this rage that I had not noticed, as I had been given high dosages of steroids for multiple sclerosis for a few years.

I went back to my room, terrified and thinking *what have I done? I'm traumatizing not only my children but their innocent friends.* I closed the door and called the advice nurse at the VA Hospital in Augusta, Georgia, where I was residing at the time. Because of my MS, the advice nurse connected me to the neurology staff on duty. While I sobbed, the nurse practitioner on my neurology team asked me questions.

"What's wrong?" she asked.

"I yelled at my son for leaving crumbs on the counter as he was preparing peanut butter and jelly sandwiches for me. I think something is wrong. I felt rage, but I know it's wrong. There's no logical reason for me to be upset about three crumbs."

"Are you going to hurt the children?"

"No, but I've never felt unbalanced like that before."

I explained that I was extremely sad that I had scared the children. The nurse told me to stay in my room, to stay calm and relaxed, and to come in Monday when I could be assessed on why I was experiencing physical rage about crumbs. She also told me to call or come in if I felt completely incontrollable, as if that was not what I had just described.

That was the first time I truly noticed that something wasn't right in my head. I had no control. Although I knew it didn't make sense, the rage that I felt inside me was so much more powerful and it overtook me. *This is not who I am. This is not real.* That's when I knew I needed help.

The following week, I had a psych evaluation assessment. The psychiatrist asked about my physical health and stressors in my life. We discussed the combination of stress from being in undergraduate school and dealing with the MS. After all of the mental and physical screenings were done, I was diagnosed with mood disorder secondary to chronic medical illness. I did a few sessions of talk therapy and was placed on medication. At this time, I had been living with MS for approximately five to six years. Since my MS diagnosis, I had already gone through a lot of life changes, but things had started to take a turn for the better. Then, all of a sudden, my brain decided to tell me I should be angry without any logical reason. I immediately recognized that I could not have anything else destroy the new norm that I had worked so hard for, so I immediately reached out for help.

On this interesting journey, I have not only accepted but embraced my diagnosis because it is one of the factors that pushes me to be successful in my career. For my personal growth, and to help others, my journey to understanding mental illness, mental wellness, and holistic health led me down a path to social work. I am now a licensed independent clinical social worker, working for the federal government of the District of Columbia as a senior social worker helping veterans. I have also worked as a social worker in homeless services and child welfare. I consider myself a skilled and seasoned social worker who has been exposed to various social work arenas, and I have thrived in them all, assisting patients who are severely mentally ill.

For us to get through to the best health, we have to be able to understand that we can't do it alone; we all need each other. What ails us ails those who are close to us. We are all connected. Throughout my journey, I have learned to share my experiences openly with anyone who cares to listen. It helps to educate others about mental health stigma and invisible disabilities like multiple sclerosis, diabetes, hypertension, lupus, and yes, mental illness. Mental illness has no look. It does not discriminate. And yes, it is a wild, unpredictable ride. But it is not a barrier to being a professional, a good parent, or a good spouse, or to having a good life. Like with most things in life, it's better to do it with help. Sometimes, you have no choice but to do it with help. Even when asking for help is not what you want to do, it is what you must do to continue forward movement in life.

Having insight into my own issues and getting assistance led me to want others to know it's okay to reach out when something is not right. We know when things are not right with ourselves, but we brush it off. We say things like "oh, we're just having an off day," but if you notice things changing in your body and your mind, the best thing to do is seek help immediately.

This experience taught me that physical and mental health go hand in hand. Although I never experienced mental illness prior to this, my experience with a chronic illness allowed me to accept my mental health concerns and diagnosis and to understand that we all need support no matter what we are dealing with in life.

Although I utilize my healthcare resources, my support networks, and my continuing education in the field of social work, I too have instances that demand that I reach out and accept support. I too have moments I can't get through alone. These are the actions I take when I'm in one of those moments and need help:

- I schedule to meet with my primary care doctor, neurologist, and mental health provider.

- I reach out to make sure nothing physical is going on that may be the cause of this change in my mental health.

- I speak with my mental health provider to discuss if changes in medication or dosage need to be considered.

- I check in with my mental health provider to process these new changes that I'm feeling.

During those times when you need to reach out for support, you have to take time to make and attend appointments. This requires you to rearrange your schedule and take time off from work, which causes additional stress, but it is necessary. When you are in a place where you know that your symptoms are spiraling and your routine is not enough, you have to reach out to your family, friends, or even colleagues to help you get it done. That may mean asking someone in your support network to give you a moment, help you set reminders, or take on additional tasks in order for you to get these things done. When you are not in control, it can be hard to accomplish daily tasks that, normally, you can do correctly and efficiently. This is when it is vital to let your support network, which includes your primary care and mental health providers, know what you are feeling. Let your family know that you need them to keep an eye out because you're feeling differently and you may need assistance keeping focus. Talk to your employer or supervisor if you are comfortable and let them know you need a mental health day or a day dedicated to self-care. Support groups and therapy are outlets for safely processing with those who have their own experiences that relate to yours. These are all positive ways to manage your wellness; however, you cannot do these things on your own when you are already frustrated and not feeling like yourself. The more you utilize these options and resources, the stigma attached to mental health and mental illness will decrease, and mental wellness will increase. Then you will know what your best health will not only look like but feel like.

Do We Dare Love the Shooter?

Lashonia Thompson-El

I know some people wonder how a person could take an-other person's life. If a child is taught to be violent, is indoc-trinated with violent values, and experiences violence inside and outside of the home, the child will be prone to violence as he or she matures. Violence is a learned behavior. Violence is a disease, and it spreads like any virus. I know because I learned to be violent. I know because I became very sick after exposure to pervasive violence. I know because I was deeply immersed in a life of violence. I was taught to carry weapons and defend myself at all costs. One awful summer night, I took someone's life. We were each nineteen years old. I land-ed myself in prison, where I would remain for eighteen years. I was a single mother, and I didn't even have a GED.

Imagine a child soldier. A young, impressionable soul who is armed with dangerous weapons and taught to slaugh-ter others who look like him or her. An inability to comply could mean death for this child. That child is me. When my parents, my siblings, and my peers taught me to defend my-self, they thought they were preparing me for survival of the fittest. I was not born violent. In fact, I was the biggest punk as a kid. I would run from fights, and I was chastised for it. My father warned me, "If anyone ever hits you, you hit them back. If you can't beat them, you pick up a bottle, a stick, or a brick, but you don't run." As he spoke these words, he held my tiny arms in a tight grip. He looked me in my eyes, and he didn't crack a smile.

Once, I ran from a group of girls into my older sister's apartment. She dragged me back outside and made me fight the first girl who stepped up. I ducked my head, closed my eyes, and started swinging. All I heard was beads falling from her braid and hitting the pavement. The final straw was when my first love grew tired of standing between me and my junior high school rivals. Eventually we saw one of the girls alone, and he pushed me forward and demanded that I fight. I was petrified. I just knew she would beat the crap out of me. I stood my ground, and from then on, I knew I had to learn to fight back. It's true what people say: "Whether or not you become good or evil depends on which part of you that you feed."

I became a monster. By the time I committed murder, I had a long history of fighting, being stabbed, and even stabbing another person. Even though I became accustomed to it, I didn't enjoy fighting. Over time, it just became habitual. I worked to build up an image that I was ready and willing to fight whoever whenever, and this helped to reduce the likelihood that I would have to fight. I also had to live up to the image.

If life is a drama, then the hood was my stage. I was performing, and my fellow actors were my male peers who had access to a lot of guns. Trapped in my need for a sense of belonging, I became the loyal sister to them. I was a person they could depend on. My apartment was a place where they could hide and stash their weapons.

Ultimately, when the judge prepared to slam his gavel, I didn't have much to say for myself. I just stood there as the curtains closed on my life. While incarcerated, I participated in trauma therapy, group therapy, and one-on-one therapy. I learned new values, I created a new normal, and I learned new ways of being. I began to study myself. I pursued my academic studies. I even converted to Islam. I also exercised a lot. For years, I ran around the track in methodic motion. Sometimes I would run for hours at a time. I transformed my life. I attacked the old me physically, mentally, spiritually, and intellectually.

My transformation process was no walk in the park, and it didn't happen overnight. There was nothing magical about it. It was painstaking work. I spent countless hours in deep reflection, praying and studying. I even began to explore the Secret and the power of intention. I read the likes of Eckhart Tolle, Les Brown, Malcolm X, and Viktor Frankl. I read *As a Man Thinketh* by James Allen, *How to Stop Worrying and Start Living* by Dale Carnegie, and every autobiography of every successful African American I could get my hands on. I was thirsty for knowledge and committed to growing and developing my true self.

Living with the choice I made to take someone's life was devastating. Almost every day I woke up, it was my first thought before I opened my eyes. As I grew to understand the meaning of life and the finality of death, I became more and more remorseful and regretful. I vowed to use my life to make a difference. I wanted to help young people learn to build empathy and change unhealthy norms, and to help those who care about young people trapped in cycles of violence understand the nuances of the violent subculture that would otherwise remain unknown.

In 2001, with ten years left to serve, I experienced several huge losses in a one-year span. It's true that death comes in threes. I lost my father when he slipped and fell down a flight of stairs. He was caring for my son at the time. I lost my younger brother to gun violence. He was murdered in SE, DC—when he was nineteen years old. One of my best friends died from an alleged overdose a few days after she was released from jail. Then, I spent forty-two days in solitary confinement for smoking a cigarette after they had been banned from the facility.

While in the hole, I became so depressed that I was worried that I would have to take psychiatric medication. The harm caused by solitary confinement cannot be emphasized enough. Lengthy periods of solitary confinement can cause hysteria, delusions, migraines, low self-esteem, depression, and more. Moreover, prolonged periods of confinement can permanently damage a person's mind, body, and spirit.

Taking psych meds was always my biggest fear. I would pray, "Oh Allah, please don't let them take my mind. They got my body, and my mind is all I have left." I knew every psychologist in every facility where I served time, and I had an open-door policy with each of them. When I was released from the hole, I had several visits with my therapist, but I wasn't feeling any better. My worry persisted.

The psychologist gave me a workbook on how to cope with depression. He told me to read it, and if I didn't feel better, we could discuss alternatives. I was more stressed out about not being able to manage my depression than I was about the actual depression. I learned in trauma treatment that sadness is not bad or wrong and should not be ignored but acknowledged and tended to. Depression was not foreign to me. I might have slept for at least five years straight when I got to the feds. Before I went into solitary confinement, I was able to manage by reading, exercising, praying, or studying. But that time in solitary hurt me mentally and emotionally, and I was really scared. I read that workbook from cover to cover, answering all the questions intently. I was overjoyed when, not long afterward, I began to feel like my old self again. I knew then that cognitive therapy could work for me, and I have continued to practice over the years.

I know firsthand that violence, just as it is learned, can be unlearned. A tendency toward violence can be managed like any other chronic disease. Learning to manage the vicarious trauma that I confront daily has saved my life. I've taken countless classes, including Alternative to Violence Project (AVP), Emotional Behavioral Therapy (EBT), Communication Conflict Resolution Program (CCRP), and Emotional Intelligence (EI). The journey to true transformation is a conflict that cannot be explained in words. The work is never-ending and daunting, but it is rewarding and inspiring. Know that you can build resistance to trauma and you can create an alternative lifestyle, even if you were born in a pervasive culture of violence.

There are several things that I know. Three of the root causes of inner-city gun violence are 1) trauma, 2) damaged self-esteem, and 3) hopelessness. Some of the solutions are simple: end bullying, provide access to education, normalize trauma-informed mental health support, and provide access to living-wage careers, suitable housing, and entrepreneurship opportunities for those who have been pushed beyond the margins of society.

One of the great challenges of our times is, how do you "treat" the child soldier? How can you empathize with and become vulnerable enough to care for the shooter? This person is reckless. They have no respect for human life. What do we do with them? If we arrest them, they will one day return to us. The trauma of incarceration will likely exacerbate their existing trauma, and their entire family will be impacted for generations to come. What's worse, the victim's family has little to no say in what they need in order to address the harm that they endured. They have lost a loved one forever, and the only solace is that the person who caused the harm will be removed from society for a long period. How can we prevent victims from becoming victims? How can we serve the shooter? The answer is simple yet complex. Young people who have been exposed to violence need trauma treatment that includes group therapy, meditation, healing circles, yoga, and storytelling. We must heal the trauma so that we can break the cycle of violence. What I know is that incarceration, like community violence, destroys the mind and spirit of those who are convicted and their families. It rips apart communities and families, causing more trauma and cyclical harm.

Reentry itself is upended by insurmountable obstacles and countless collateral consequences. Some formerly incarcerated people will suffer for past choices "from the gavel to the grave." If the purpose of the justice system is to merely punish, then we are on the right track, but if we want to prevent violence, we need some transformative justice solutions. When working with young people, we must continue to ask "What happened to you?" and not just "What did you do?" The way to build empathy is to help young people unpack and build resilience to trauma.

In the past decade since my release, I overcame homelessness, completed my bachelor's degree, and married the man of my dreams. I have worked in reentry, prison conditions, restorative justice, and gun violence prevention. My absolute biggest challenge has been family reunification. When I landed myself in prison, my daughter was three years old and my son was an infant. By the time I was released after serving eighteen years in prison, my children were young adults. My daughter was angry. She suffers with severe post-traumatic stress disorder (PTSD). Now she is a mother of five children, and my deepest desire is to break the generational cycle of violence and incarceration within my family. We are a work in progress. We have tried counseling and mediation. Mindfulness and restorative practices like healing circles and yoga have been more beneficial for us. We have been blessed to work with some of the elders in DC who are leading healing practitioners, including Ivy Hylton and Ayanna Gregory.

In 2019, my daughter became a trauma-informed yoga expert and introduced me to the practice. When I was incarcerated, I was a fitness junkie, but after I came home, over time, I began to run less often. Eventually, I stopped working out altogether. Once I was introduced to yoga, I began to get to know my body all over again. It did wonders for my stress management.

It feels good to have an array of tools I can use to manage my trauma. I'm no longer chained to the values that were passed down to me. Today, not only do I practice yoga regularly, but my exercise routine in general is rather consistent. I attribute my ability to handle daily stress to my yoga and mindfulness practices. Working with Ayanna and Ivy allowed me and my family to engage in talk therapy, music therapy, aromatherapy, and meditation. Our work with Dr. Bruce Purnell of the Love More Movement is based on a transformative justice and healing framework, and it has been most helpful in my post-incarceration development. Understanding leadership and learning to practice the principle of love are the foundations of Moorish science. I was drawn to Dr. Purnell's Afrocentric perspective on what it means to truly be liberated. Dr. Purnell encouraged me to continue to go against the grain and unplug often. He helped me realize I can be me and pursue my goals without following the norms around me. He confirmed for me that it is okay to be different. He encouraged me to dig deeper and to "dream like I never had a nightmare." He is one of my biggest inspirations.

I am also inspired by the work of Dr. Joy Leary. She writes about the impact of post-traumatic slave syndrome (PTSS) and how some of the survival strategies our people developed during slavery cause us harm today. Developing my consciousness has enabled me to manage my mental health.

I am inspired by the WIRE: Women Involved in Reentry Efforts. The WIRE is a network of formerly incarcerated women who have successfully reintegrated back into society. They are peer advocates and peer mentors to women in prison and women returning home from incarceration. The women of the WIRE are trained social workers, outreach workers, violence interrupters, public speakers, authors, restorative justice facilitators, peer specialists, and more. I rely heavily on peer support from the women I served time with, and the WIRE has proven that having the support of someone who shares your lived experience can help you successfully navigate life after release. None of the women of the WIRE have been reincarcerated.

I am also inspired by the women of the CURE the Streets team here in DC. They are the backbone of their families and they are the minority in their workforce. These women serve as program managers, violence interrupters, and outreach workers for gun violence prevention sites in various high-risk neighborhoods throughout the city. They are my sheroes. They have the credibility, influence, and key relationships necessary to build trust and prevent violence in the

DC neighborhoods that suffer the most. They are skilled at detecting violence, mediating conflicts, and changing norms.

These people who inspire me—the therapists, the scholars, the healers, the women of CURE the Streets, and the women of the WIRE—all have decided, consciously or subconsciously, to dare love the shooter. It is no wonder why. In the words of Dr. Martin Luther King Jr., "Darkness cannot drive out darkness; only light can do that. Hate cannot drive out hate; only love can do that. Hate multiplies hate, violence multiplies violence, and toughness multiplies toughness in a descending spiral of destruction."

Undiagnosed Hood Disease: A Root Cause of Inner-City Violence

Sean Thompson-El

My story is not a unique one; it is happening all over the country. I was born in St. Louis, Missouri, in a rough inner-city neighborhood called the "Ville." I grew up during the war on drugs and the era of mass incarceration, among poverty and normalized criminal behavior. Like many other American youth, I was traumatized and highly infected by the disease of violence. My social environment caused me to suffer "hood trauma." This is a form of post-traumatic stress disorder (PTSD), and it is real. The African American community has long looked at mental illness as somewhat of a taboo and has come to accept violence as normal behavior—but this trauma of being born and raised in impoverished neighborhoods, with high unemployment, high crime, and poor health conditions is proven to have lasting effects.

I was diagnosed with PTSD approximately nine years ago. It was not until I conducted my own research and corroborated my findings with my therapist that we concluded that it was highly possible that I had been suffering from an undiagnosed case of severe PTSD for over twenty-five years. PTSD is a psychiatric disorder that can occur in people who have experienced or witnessed traumatic events such as a violent personal assault, war or combat, rape, or other events. The symptoms of PTSD are many and are displayed in patients in a multitude of different ways, from obvious and outrageous to subtle and hard to recognize. Symptoms include anger, paranoia, hypervigilance, anxiety, drug abuse, depression, isolation, flashbacks, and nightmares. As far back as I can remember, I have experienced some form of symptomatic behavior of this mental health disease. These symptoms were normalized, and my behavior was accepted in the community. I was just another angry, bad kid. Me being traumatized and suffering PTSD was never even considered.

As a youth, I had many traumatic experiences, but I must say for the most part my childhood was good. I lived in a working-class neighborhood and attended Catholic school—until I was expelled from all parochial schools. I played sports and had lots of fun growing up.

My mother was a top-notch booster and heroin addict. She was in and out of prison as far back as I can remember, so my great-grandmother and grandmother were primarily responsible for my upbringing. I must admit they raised me well. At a very young age, the importance of family and integrity was instilled in me. My grandmother was a functioning alcoholic who drank until she passed out every night. For over thirty years, she awoke every morning to go to work for the city government. She had her faults, but her love for my siblings and me never faltered.

I was decent in sports, but I excelled academically in school. After I was expelled from parochial schools in maybe the fourth or fifth grade, I began attending St. Louis public schools. I was at least a grade or two ahead of the rest of the class. At the time, I didn't quite understand how privileged I had been to be educated in a private school setting with smaller classrooms and more attentive teachers. I'm not sure when or how the fighting began, but I was the new kid from Catholic school who sat up front with the smart kids. So I fought. I fought kids in the morning time. I fought kids at recess and again after school. I don't know if this was some type of childhood initiation or the development of the pecking order. All I know is I fought, and I fought hard. It couldn't get back to my grandmother or siblings that I got my ass kicked and didn't fight back.

Today, as an adult, I reflect on how ruthless and violent I was as a youth and how this violence was not only accepted but applauded. The normalization of violence in depressed communities is not a new phenomenon. The narrative that inner cities are places where random acts of violence occur is false. I grew up within a subculture where daily violence occurred, and one was either predator or prey. There was no middle ground. I saw my first dead body when I was maybe twelve years old. I was involved in my first violent crime at maybe fourteen. When you are a kid from the inner city, you learn to mask your emotions and live with your trauma. I became adept at putting my fears aside and locking my traumas deep inside my psyche.

Through counseling, I learned that the most stressful and agitating times during my youth were going to see my mother (Gee-Gee) in prison. My grandmother religiously forced us to visit her on a monthly basis. Those visits used to have me anxious and stressed out. Not only would there be several fights with kids in the neighborhood when I returned home from visiting my "jailbird momma," but the guards, the barbed wire, and the shadow of doom seemed to consume me.

My relationship with Gee-Gee was precarious. On one hand, she was cool; when she was home, she allowed me to smoke weed and never really disciplined me about fighting or getting suspended from school. But on the flip side, she would get on her concerned-parent soapbox, telling me she heard I was dealing drugs, carrying guns, and fronting in front of my grandmother. All the times I had smuggled balloons of Valium and marijuana into prison for her and she was trashing me in front of my grandma like I'm some villain, when in actuality, she was my coconspirator.

To say Gee-Gee was not a major influencer as I developed into a full-fledged criminal would be a lie. Gee-Gee was a top-flight hustler, and everyone knew her. Being Gee-Gee's son opened some infamous doors. But I will add that every criminal endeavor or violent crime I committed was done by my own volition. I've always been an alpha, not easily influenced by anyone. As I grew into adolescence, my fighting became more brutal and vicious. I recall one time when one of Gee-Gee's boyfriends slapped her and took her car. When my friends and I finally caught up with him, he was nonchalant about the situation. He hadn't taken heed of the warning that my friends and I were looking for him. He had no idea we weren't ordinary kids. Word got back to us that he was at a bar, getting drunk and talking trash. It was four of us. None of us weighed more than 150 pounds, and nobody was older than fifteen years old. He was a big dude, the wannabe tough guy type. I walked straight up to the dude and demanded the car keys. He smirked, and before he could get a word out, we rushed him. A couple of us had knives, so he was hurt really bad. The only reason that we didn't kill him was because the OG called us off and demanded us to "go and take all of your clothes and weapons and burn them."

As I reflect, I can see how my mental illness progressed and was amplified by my criminal lifestyle. At fifteen years old, I was doing a lot of self-medicating by smoking weed, taking Valium, and drinking daily. The symptoms of my PTSD were more pronounced. I was always paranoid, watching my back, anxious, hypervigilant, and easily triggered into violence. Around this time, I was convicted of a violent crime in juvenile court. I had stabbed another kid. I was found to be a delinquent in juvenile court and sent to a group home.

My reputation had preceded me, so I didn't have but a couple of fights; plus, I excelled academically, and the counselors always wanted to show off my test scores. They let me get away with a lot of stuff that was against the rules. This place was a breeding ground for sex offenders. There was always something kinky going on in the bathroom among both the residents and staff. As a rehabilitation center for youth, it was a joke. Ninety days after I was released from the group home, I was involved in another violent altercation. I stabbed someone else, and this time I was sent to a juvenile reformatory. This was where they sent all the bad kids from the state of Missouri. It was gladiator training. You either knew how to fight, or someone was going to rape you or take your food. These acts were normalized and done openly. I won't say it was condoned by staff, but I never saw staff do anything to stop a rape, molestation, or robbery. I was never psychiatrically evaluated, although I do recall a few dudes being prescribed Thorazine because they had tried to escape a few times, and they kept them highly medicated.

Today, I look back and I'm saddened at how the system treated us as youth. The trauma that we as children experienced was obvious. For the most part, it was all in our files, and if not, definitely in our behaviors. No one thought we were worth saving. And so, as it is with all juvenile offenders in the state of Missouri, I was released six months prior to my seventeenth birthday.

Ninety days after my seventeenth birthday, I was charged and eventually convicted of second degree murder and sentenced to twenty-five years in prison. During my criminal proceeding, at no time was I psychologically evaluated or seen by a psychiatrist. In no way am I attempting to minimize my behavior. My crime was reckless and violent. I am merely making an assessment from a clinical perspective. How can a youth who has a documented history of aggressive and violent behavior not be seen by a clinician to evaluate his mental health?

I served exactly thirteen years and two months of my twenty-five-year sentence before I was released on parole.

During that incarceration, I spent eight and a half years in supermax. This place was brutal and violent. It exacerbated my trauma to a severe stage. From May 1984 to October 1984, there were over 180 stabbings and four murders in this maximum-security unit. The conditions were so unconscionable that the federal government shut down that section of the prison.

The entire maximum-security unit was filled with men with symptomatic behavior. Everyone was paranoid, hypervigilant, and potentially manic. At one point, I was beaten unmercifully by prison guards and placed in an isolation cell. I was on "no contact," twenty-four-hour lockdown. I lived in total isolation for two and a half years and was only released after I filed a federal civil complaint. I was awarded a settlement of $9,000 for excessive use of force and the violation of my civil rights.

When I was released from prison, nothing about my behavior had changed. In fact, I lasted in free society for a mere twenty months before I was charged with federal drug and weapons charges and sentenced to fifteen years. I was transferred to a maximum-security federal prison in Kansas. Two days after being on the yard, another violent incident occurred. I was placed under investigation for attempted murder and spent another year in an isolation cell. I was only thirty-two years old, and I had already spent close to half of my life in prison. I knew then that I had to learn to control my temper and reinvent myself, or I would die in prison.

Although I didn't realize it at the time, I was self-isolating and avoiding all types of confrontation. By this time, I knew that I had some type of anxiety disorder. I was always stressed and on the brink of exploding. I began a regimen of weight training, calisthenics, and cardio. I re-embraced my faith and made a conscious effort to avoid the people, places, and things that could trigger me into violence. I was released again from prison after serving thirteen years and seven months.

I did not return to St. Louis. I relocated to Chicago, enrolled in college, and began working on reinventing myself. As part of my supervised release, I was required to attend drug treatment classes. I missed a couple of meetings due to my class schedule and not having the resources to travel back and forth across town. I was in a meeting with my parole officer, and she triggered me. She was pressing me about drug classes. I exploded. I went from zero to a hundred in about five seconds. I told her point blank, "I'm not going to no more drug treatment and I'm not paying to sit in group therapy with a bunch of crackheads. Send me back to jail or whatever."

"You don't have to go to anymore drug treatment," she said. "Will you go and see a therapist for me? I think you have severe PTSD and you need to get that checked out."

This was the first time that anyone had spoken to me about my mental health. I was in the system for over thirty years, and my parole officer—who is not a trained clinician—diagnosed me.

My first therapy session was one of the most enlightening and informative conversations that I have ever had. My therapist was the first person I ever heard use the term "hood trauma." She spoke about how I had been traumatized pre- and post-incarceration. She further explained that I was not crazy but suffering from a mental illness and that certain situations could trigger me into violent outbursts. I sat there smiling. Someone had just explained to me the things I had been trying to figure out for years. I was thrilled not to be crazy or a maniac. I took to my weekly therapy sessions vigorously. I wanted to know all I could about PTSD and trauma. The fact that I was in my forties and had never been told about this disease was mind-boggling. I learned that exercising daily was the best thing I could do for my stress and anxieties. I also learned that what I thought was standoffish behavior was a way of self-isolating. These symptoms were normal considering the chronic, complex trauma I had endured and it's long-lasting impact on my mental health.

Many youth are born into misfortune through no fault of their own. Many have never felt love or compassion. Being labeled as a hoodlum and a thug is just as detrimental to a kid's psyche as drugs and alcohol. The world has become totally punitive and unforgiving. The war on drugs and mass incarceration have caused many in society to forget about the most vulnerable victims—the children. Society has programmed us to believe that these young Black and Brown youth are incorrigible monsters. These youth suffer with severe mental illness triggered by the trauma of growing up in the hood.

Today, I am a graduate of the University of Illinois in Chicago. I hold a master of arts in criminology, law, and justice with a concentration in violent studies. My primary field of study is youth gangs, the root causes of violence, and violence prevention. I live in Washington, DC, where I have worked in assertive community treatment (ACT) and mental health crisis intervention for the past six years. Through the lens of a mental health professional (MHP), I am trained to conduct mental health assessments. On a daily basis, when I interact with men and boys in the neighborhoods across the city, I make observations that reflect symptomatic behavior consistent with severe PTSD. I remain in therapy, and intense exercise is still one of the best ways I've learned to eliminate stress. I have added mindfulness, meditation, yoga, and gardening to my self-care strategies. As an advocate against gun violence, I meet regularly with high-risk youth and speak candidly about my mental health issues and experiences with therapy. I've learned to live with my disease and embrace change. I am dedicated to preventing gun violence, educating communities of color about mental health, and eradicating racism in our country—because BLACK YOUTH LIVES really do MATTER.

Recognition

Michael Young

I should have recognized the behavior. The off-color remarks, the chilled bottles of vodka in the freezer, the evidence of racing thoughts, and the other signs that meet the criteria for bipolar disorder. My family and I watched her behavior for years without intervention, not because of unintelligence, but due to lack of awareness and to mental health not being focused on during this particular time period. Family members always said, "She's just crazy!" when she acted out at family functions. The resulting death of my family member did not enlighten us to mental health. We just focused on the fact she drank herself to death.

Mental health would become the focus within my family many years later. However, before the intense focus on mental health by the country, I served in the United States Marine Corps (USMC) without a mental health breakdown. When I was accused of an aggressive action and made to attend an anger management class, I sat among others like me, some of whom I believe should have just received counseling instead of being persecuted for their situation. Was I angry? Of course I was angry! There were situations occurring in my life I had to deal with.

That year, 1993, continued to be fraught with complications, as anger came into play once again because of the same life situations. I was an end-of-service United States Marine who was a Primary Marksmanship Instructor (I taught on the rifle range), held a Private Investigator license, and had the ability to carry a concealed weapon if needed. The same situation that landed me in anger management class resulted in my incarceration. Due to my military background, using mace on anyone, seemingly unprovoked, was an assault. For someone who thought of themselves as highly intelligent, standing in front of a judge, without representation, and pleading guilty to assault was not a situation I ever thought I would be in. My knees buckled as the judge took ten seconds—yes, only ten seconds—to sentence me to one year in jail. My family was not aware as I was led to lockup, awaiting transport to 911 East City Jail in Norfolk, Virginia, to begin my sentence.

Not being aware of local sentencing laws (this will come into play later), I hunkered down and resigned myself to a year away from the outside world—but my family, who had not had contact with me for over one week, tracked me down, and I was bailed out and returned to Washington, DC, to await my appeal. I returned to Norfolk, Virginia, for my appeal, which was upheld. I came to learn there was a law on the books called the half and half law. Basically, my sentence was cut in half twice, and I served three months of the one-year sentence.

Upon release, I once again returned to Washington, DC. I was able to work various jobs, which allowed me to enjoy the nightlife. The term "night owl" was very prevalent as I was growing up, however, I soon learned the term "insomniac." As it turns out, I had been an insomniac since I was a child. My best friend used to call me a vampire. I laugh about his labeling now, but I look back on everything I have done or said, and understand what has occurred in my life.

Not knowing I had a mental illness and not receiving treatment made me focus differently. I adapted several coping mechanisms, which are harmful for those of us who have been diagnosed with bipolar disorder. I did not like taking pills, even in pain, but I would drink excessively. It is called drowning your brain. For those of us who experience constant highs and energy, it is a way of leveling off. The depressant helps to curtail the multiple thoughts taking place at once—but it does not stop the behavior. I continued on my path of self-destruction for a while. I still cannot remember six months of my life from drowning my brain. The racing thoughts continued, and I convinced myself I was okay.

My intellect allowed me to function at several lucrative jobs, and then eventually have a meaningful relationship. My relationship turned to marriage, but things were not aligned correctly. One day, my brother-in-law told me something was not right. I needed help! I was asked, if help could be obtained, would I accept the help? I responded yes to his inquiry. I was giving lip service. Five minutes later, I received a call from him, and I remember the conversation to this day:

"You are a Vet. I called the Veterans Administration, and they have a program for you!"

"F@@K!"

Yes, that is what I said! I just knew he would fail. However, he cared enough to make the effort, and succeeded.

Keeping my word, I went to the Veterans Administration. It was the best move I had ever made!

I was able to maintain my relationship with my wife and go to counseling and treatment. At first, I was reluctant when sharing what I was feeling with other men in a room. I had been through the experience in anger management class years before. The fact there was a nurse practitioner heading the sessions really upset me. I thought, *Here comes the judgment again!* My previous experience with counseling clouded my viewpoint. Looking back, it was the fact I felt a woman was judging a man no matter what may have happened at the time, which occurred in anger management class. Eventually, I warmed to these sessions and participated, and became aware I had a diagnosis after submitting to an assessment. I dropped my guard and was open to medication management.

Once I accepted my diagnosis, I realized what had been happening for years. I became aware of mental health and what was required to maintain my survival. I would be no good to anyone else if I was not good to myself. I soon realized I could overcome my racing thoughts when there was something I was extremely interested in. My concentration on those subjects would be laser focused. But what about those events in my life I was not extremely interested in? The United States Marine Corps (USMC) provided extreme focus, and now therapy was my new focus. I started a medication regimen. I began facilitating groups and helping my fellow service members. I soon was approached about becoming a peer specialist.

I was not sure about becoming a peer specialist. I had previously not been a fan of talking about my feelings, but how was I going to get other men or women to open up about what they were experiencing? However, I took the chance. I applied to the Department of Mental Health (DMH) and was accepted out of multiple candidates. I like to think I interview well. There was a stipend, which worked, but really did not matter. I had, and have, a great support system in my wife and family. I approached my new endeavor like I approached the Marine Corps: be the best! I studied all hours of the day to understand mental health and what it meant for me. I learned more than I wanted to.

I was a textbook person with bipolar disorder, with one exception. I did not become depressed. I could constantly feel the energy, which resulted in not having an off button. This came in handy while studying to become a peer specialist and would play an integral part in work after completing the course. I was able to complete my field practicum with a crisis unit, become a contractor, and then become an essential full-time employee with the Department of Behavioral Health. Along the way, I was able to work in the Department of Corrections (DOC). Working in the DOC has fueled a new passion: obtaining a degree in forensic psychology.

My focus while doing crisis work is on individuals diagnosed with mental health conditions, substance use, or co-occurring disorders who were incarcerated and returning to the community. Returning citizens have a percentage significantly greater than the average citizenry to be reincarcerated or complete suicide. Due to this high percentage, returning citizens and so-called supportive systems face disastrous outcomes. Returning citizens receive mental health treatment while incarcerated but have far less access to mental health services and become entangled in an ongoing cycle of being reincarcerated and fulfilling multiple sentences. The desired remedy requires treatment focused on recovery and delivering continuous transcendence services assisting a returning citizen into the community. Returning citizens can benefit from programs conducted by peers starting before release. Plans for release and a warm handoff to prearranged community mental health services provide support, stemming the tide of reincarceration. How can mental health become addressed properly without personal involvement by a society that has a tenet based on religious freedom and a belief in God?

I believe I have had a unique experience and show that ongoing treatment works. Once I was stabilized, I began regular psychiatric visits and still see a therapist twice a month. It has become easy to discuss my feelings and what is going on in my life. Therapy has become essential in my life due to working in a crisis unit. I hear what everyone else is going through and can feel like I am holding the weight of the world on my shoulders. There must be a healthy outlet, and talking to my therapist allows the very outlet needed. Having a supportive family also provides another outlet. There is no judgment. There is no threat of stigma. My diagnosis does not define me.

Trust on Trial

Anthony Jerome McAllister

It is not about getting over losing my daughter;
more importantly, it is about learning to live
with what I now call my new normal!

"Trust God" was a phrase that I was taught as a youth in Sunday school and in Christian education youth training. It was instilled in me by my parents, who were deeply vested in their faith. I received these teachings but handled them matter-of-factly. I tended to stake claim to the words "I trust God" as convenient words of responses to something, rather than as words of resolution for something. Life would, indeed, teach me to put my trust on trial as I learned to trust God.

As I pen this chapter, I dedicate it to the life and memory of my baby daughter, Ayana Jazmyn McAllister, and to my parents, the late Minister Theodore James and Mrs. Sallie Lyon McAllister. I honor my parents, who were the epitome of greatness, beginning with their union. You see, each parent brought eight children to their union, added two children from their union (my brother and me), and adopted three grandchildren. Wait! Not all of the children lived under the same roof at the same time.

With the merger of a family unit of this magnitude, McAllister-Sanders, trust was constantly on trial in terms of who and what to trust. With God in the midst, we were blessed to be one big happy family, enjoying many memorable family unions. One of the most valuable lessons that my parents instilled in my siblings and me was to always put God first and trust Him in all we do. We continue to witness the fruit of what they taught us and what they modeled. As a youth, I did not readily grasp the meaning of always trusting God in everything, but as I grew from a teenager to an adult, life would prove to be my greatest teacher. The true test of my trusting God occurred in 2017 in a fatal occurrence.

The natural course of life's journey is that children will bury their parents. This was not the natural course for my wife and me. On March 21, 2017, we lost our beautiful eighteen-year-old daughter, Ayana, to random handgun violence. My two daughters, N'Daja and Ayana, college freshmen, were enjoying an evening with friends in our nation's capital while home on spring break. On March 20, 2017, at 8:40 p.m., the unthinkable happened.

Random shots struck my daughter and grazed her college roommate's shoulder. The hospital cleaned Ayana's roommate's wound, and, thank God, she was released to go home. Ayana lived approximately thirteen hours, and the next morning, she entered into eternal rest.

My heart aches each time I think of the loss of my youngest daughter. As a parent, you nurture, protect, and guide your children as you prepare them for a life of independence, a life that affords them survival tools for well-being and success. Ayana's death literally took the life out of me. The unknown perpetrator responsible for her death robbed us of Ayana's love and the purpose God had ordained for her. For Ayana, there would be no college graduation, no marriage, no children, no grandchildren. I continue to ask God to heal the pain I experience when I think of what Ayana and my family were robbed of.

This situation clearly tested my faith and put my trust on trial. Ayana was a beautiful, goofy, fun-loving, sweet, and compassionate young lady who was destined for greatness. Upon graduation from high school in 2016, Ayana participated in the Maryland State Troopers Cadet Program. She was excited about going off to college to major in criminal justice and pursuing a career in law enforcement as a detective. She was scheduled to graduate from college in June 2020. As June 2020 came and went, I grieved for what could have been: Ayana's graduation from college and the pursuit of her dreams. Grieving takes time; that is why I remain patient with my healing process.

The loss of a loved one can be one of life's most devastating and stressful events. It can cause major emotional crises and, if gone unchecked, can literally wipe you out. That is why it is important to practice self-care when things are calm, so that when a crisis occurs, you can handle it with minimal stress.

As a younger person, I witnessed both of my parents lose children to death. I watched as they mourned their loss in their own respective way, but the one common denominator in each case was their unwavering faith and belief. They trusted the God of All Comfort to never leave nor forsake them, to heal their pain and make their grieving bearable. Gun-related fatalities have played a multifaceted role in the life of my family.

My daughter's untimely death clearly tested my faith. For a split second, it entered my mind to put God on trial, and ask Him, "How could you allow this to happen to my family who has served you faithfully?" Unlike my wife, during our many local and national television interviews, I was not ready to say to the perpetrator(s), as she did, "I forgive you" for murdering our baby. It is testing times like these when you have to intentionally trust God, despite the devil telling you to quit on God because He has failed you. In these moments, I choose to continue to trust God and believe that He will see me through. Today, I do not dwell on the person(s) responsible for my daughter's death but remember the words of Jesus, "Vengeance is mine; I will repay, saith the Lord" (Romans 12:19). I admit that it has been a work in progress. I know that there will still be dark days ahead, but in spite of the dark days, I will continue to love God and love my neighbor.

During dark moments in our lives, we may choose to isolate and withdraw from everyone. Realizing that God has promised, "Never will I leave you; never will I forsake you" (Hebrews 13:5 NIV), it is a blessing to have human resources that can fellowship and minister to us. My church family has been a blessed spiritual resource of healing for my family. Being a part of the Galilee Deacons and men's ministries is a great source of inspiration. These spiritual connections made the load lighter during our down times. Spending time with praying men fed my faith. Additionally, family, friends, and fraternity, (the three Fs), were and still are sources of strength and support. There is much to say about God's gift to me, that my family, siblings, cousins, nieces, and nephews continue to be attentive and assure that there is no lack of love.

John 16:33 reminds us that tribulation will come in our lives. Yet, the good news is that God, the Son, through calvary, has overcome the world. If you are in an estranged relationship with God, family, or others, I challenge you to lay aside all petty differences, weights that hinder you from running this race of life. God has gifted us with family who can be a special support that we truly need. Friends who have been confidants and provide support can prove to be invaluable during this major crisis in your life. Although fraternity may not be a part of your life, I must highlight my fraternity brothers for their love and support of my family and me. The motto for my illustrious Omega Psi Fraternity is "Friendship is Essential to the Soul." During my time of bereavement, the fraternity of brotherhood showed the true meaning of this motto.

I am further reminded of the dark, dark moment when my wife and I were at the cemetery making burial arrangements for our daughter's final earthly resting place. In this moment, my mind went into overdrive. I was thinking, "Where is she? Who is taking care of my baby's remains?" In that very moment of concern, my phone rang, and the person on the other end greeted me with, "Hello *Brother* McAllister." This greeting immediately let me know that it was a fraternity brother. He said, "This is Brother James Locke, and I'm one of the assistant medical examiners for the State of Maryland. I want you to know that I am taking care of your daughter, and I will treat her as if she were my own daughter." In that moment of trust on trial, God spoke perfect peace to my soul. This was God using an ordinary person to do an extraordinary thing that blessed my family. Proverbs 3:5-6 NIV reminds us to trust and never doubt God: "Trust in the Lord with all your heart and lean not on your own understanding; in all your ways submit to him, and he will make your paths straight."

When we doubt God, that is when He shows up to let us know He is still working it out for our good. His track record is evidence that God is an on-time God, yes, He is! If you have people who God has placed in your life, allow them to be a source of support to you in your time of need. God uses ordinary people to do extraordinary things!

While God works in our crises through family, friends, and fraternity, I highly recommend therapy as another source of support. It is important to lay aside every stigma that may be attached to therapy and embrace this God-given tool. Many may declare that you can "pray crises away," but Scripture reminds us, "thus also Faith by itself, if it does not have works, is dead. (James 2:17 NKJV).

Let me confess—I entered therapy a bit apprehensive. Perhaps it was because of the stigma unfairly attached to therapy. Since my daughter was murdered in Washington, DC, I was offered therapy through crime victims, and the therapy has proven to be quite valuable to me in many ways. I took the opportunity, not because I was in a dark place at that particular time, but because I knew that later dark times would revisit me. I was paired with a therapist and, immediately, we connected on a number of levels.

What I have discovered over the past two years from therapy is that it can be helpful for situations other than grief. For the first time, I am able to be totally vulnerable about various aspects of my life. Not only does therapy help me to alleviate feelings of grief and loss, but it helps me chart a road map for life going forward. If you are reading this chapter and you or someone you know is at a crossroads and unsure of the direction to take, I strongly urge you to consider therapy. Therapy, in conjunction with faith, can prove to be helpful.

Not a day goes by that I do not think of Ayana. Losing a child or someone you love, under any circumstance, can put you on an emotional roller coaster. My wife and I decided early on that we needed to focus on positive goals and objectives that would honor our daughter's memory, be therapeutic for us, and be of service to others. The Ayana J. McAllister Legacy Foundation was birthed out of this decision. The mission of the Ayana J. McAllister Legacy Foundation is "to deliberately engage communities of color disproportionately impacted by gun violence through advocacy and educational strategies." The foundation has provided scholarship money to deserving high school graduates. It is our sincere hope through this foundation to significantly reduce incidents of homicide, suicide, and acts of violence resulting from the irresponsible use of firearms by high-risk individuals.

On March 21, 2018, the community where Ayana was killed, Fort Chaplin in Washington, DC, honored Ayana's memory by naming a wing in its new state-of-the-art community center, the Ayana J. McAllister Education Center. Our daughter's memory has been honored in so many ways.

As I am blessed to awaken each morning to witness the rising of the sun and the going down of the same, I thank God for the gifts of our two daughters and the blessing of fatherhood. God has also sent us a beloved grandson, Zyir, who fills our heart with love and hope. Circumstances in my life have caused me to intentionally strive to plan devotional time with God, make healthy life-changing decisions, and meet deadlines in my spiritual and secular servanthood life. By God's Hand, my faith and therapy allow me to praise God in all things.

Thank you for reading my story. It is my prayer that you will allow your faith and therapy to help you put your trust on trial as you face crises that are sure to come in your life. They will come!

Appendix

Addiction affects 19.7 million American individuals ages twelve and older, according to SAMHSA.gov. It is a brain disease that is manifested by compulsive substance use despite negative and often harmful consequences. The term "addiction" means compulsive physiological need for and use of habit-forming substances. Those who suffer from this challenging condition (severe substance use disorder) have an intense focus on using certain substances, including but not limited to alcohol and drugs, to the point that it impacts every area of their lives. Substance abuse disorders or addictions can present as distorted thinking, bizarre and sometimes criminal behavior, drug cravings, and poor judgment and decision-making. Continued substance use often results in poor health outcomes, problems with memory and learning, and impaired judgment. Substance abuse is treatable, and those affected can recover.

Anxiety disorders affect approximately 264 million people in the United States. It is estimated that more than 30 percent of American adults experience anxiety disorder at some time in their lives, according to the World Health Organization. Mild forms of anxiety are a normal part of life and not related to a mental illness. Anxiety is one of the most common forms of mental illness. There is a high correlation between this disorder and physical health problems. Anxiety disorders are expressed by intense, excessive, and persistent worry and fear about everyday situations. For some, anxiety disorders can be debilitating.

Bipolar disorder affects 46 million people around the world, according to Our World in Data. Previously referred to as manic depression, bipolar disorder is a mood disorder that causes radical shifts in mood, energy, and the ability to function. Individuals with this diagnosis may have depressive and manic episodes. The depressive episode can cause a person to feel sad, experience low energy, and have low to no motivation, while manic episodes cause a person to feel extreme energy, optimism, and euphoria. The intensity of symptoms varies. There is a high correlation of bipolar disorder and substance abuse and co-occurring health conditions. While there is no cure for bipolar disorder, treatment is available to help individuals manage symptoms and behaviors. While there is no cure for bipolar disorder, treatment is available to help individuals manage symptoms and behaviors, with a combination of medication and various therapies.

Depression is among the most common mental illnesses and the cause of the most serious health problems in the United States, affecting close to 300 million people of all ages worldwide, according to the World Health Organization. A diagnosis of depression is often misunderstood and is vastly different than feeling sad or disappointed by life challenges; it is a serious and often debilitating mood disorder that impacts how people function daily. Depression can be long-lasting and can range in intensity from mild to severe. Severe depression can lead to suicide, as close to 800,000 people die from suicide each year. Suicide is the second-leading cause of death in young adults. Depression is the leading cause of disability in the United States among adults.

Grief is the acute pain that accompanies loss. Grief can be complicated by how the loss—such as a murder, loss of a child, or divorce, among others—occurred and is compounded by feelings of guilt and confusion, especially if the relationship was difficult. Grief can mirror depression, as there is a presence of sadness, a "loss of capacity for pleasure; insomnia; and a loss of interest in eating or taking care of oneself," according to *Psychology Today*. Some people in their despair contemplate suicide after a loss. For some, grief never goes away, but people learn to manage a new normal with time.

Post-Traumatic Stress Disorder, more commonly called PTSD, develops in people who have experienced a dangerous or traumatic event that triggered intense fear. Approximately, 8 percent of the population are affected by PTSD, which is manifested by experiences in both cognitive and mood symptoms, including but not limited to feeling stressed or scared even when they are not in danger, according to the National Center for PTSD with the US Department of Veterans Affairs. Some people will experience short-term symptoms, while others will develop chronic symptoms, impacting their ability to function. PTSD is often experienced by re-experiencing the symptoms, reactivity, flashbacks, bad dreams, and frightening thoughts associated with the triggering event.

Schizophrenia is a serious chronic mental illness that affects the way a person thinks, feels, and behaves. Schizophrenia is less common than other mental illnesses, affecting approximately 2.6 million adults over age eighteen in the United States, according to the Treatment Advocacy Center. People with schizophrenia often experience thought disturbances, which can result in hallucinations and delusions, causing a difficulty distinguishing between what is real and what is a delusion; may be severely "unresponsive or withdrawn; and may have difficulty expressing normal emotions in social situations," according to Different Brains. There is no cure for schizophrenia; however, there are promising and effective treatments. Left untreated, the symptoms can be persistent and disabling. Approximately 40 percent of individuals with schizophrenia go untreated, according to the Treatment Advocacy Center.

Sponsors

The Ayana J. McAllister Foundation,

a nonprofit organization whose mission is to deliberately engage communities of color disproportionately impacted by gun violence through advocacy and education strategies

In March of 2017, cofounders Anthony J. and Tyreese R. McAllister founded the 501(c)3 after their eighteen-year-old daughter Ayana was killed by gun violence while she and her sister, N'Daja, were home on spring break from college. Having lived a life of public service and ministry, the McAllisters quickly went into action, triumphing over the tragedy. The foundation's intention is to contribute to the significant reduction of acts of homicide, suicide, and violence that result from irresponsible use of firearms in Black and Brown communities.

Learn more at www.ayanamcallister.com

***

Clinical & Forensic Associates,
a private counseling and consulting firm

Our professional team of therapists work with individuals, couples, and families facing one of many of life's challenges, including but not limited to depression, anxiety, trauma history, or current crisis. We strive to improve the emotional well-being of clients by providing collaborative and client-focused therapeutic services that align with the belief that the client is the expert in his or her own life but desires to identify and address current and long-standing difficulties, as well as experience more joy and alleviate suffering and self-defeating thoughts and behaviors.

Learn more at www.clinicalforensicassociates.com

About the Authors

Tyreese R. McAllister is a licensed mental health practitioner with over twenty-five years of experience in the field of emergency mental health, helping individuals who have experienced crisis and traumatic events to recover and overcome through radical resilience.

After earning her master's degree in counseling psychology and a postmaster's certificate in addictions counseling from Johns Hopkins University, Tyreese became credentialed as a criminal justice addictions professional, licensed as a professional counselor, and certified as a clinical supervisor. She is also a certified sex offender treatment professional and certified clinical trauma specialist who has extensive forensic and disaster preparedness, recovery, and response training and experience.

Among her many accolades, Tyreese was awarded The Good Neighbor Award, Prince George's County State's Attorney Award, and the Sister's 4 Sister Circle of Grace Award. Author of *Is My Lollipop in Heaven?* and coauthor of *Soul Talk, Vol. 3*, she currently resides in Upper Marlboro, Maryland.

Learn more at www.tyreesemcallister.org

Dr. Reneé Allen is the host of the *Reneé Allen & Friends Show,* cohost of the *Chris Thomas Show with Dr. Reneé,* and correspondent for *Sister 2 Sister 2.0 with Jamie Foster Brown.* As the vice president of media for Global Health Solutions, she is in partnership with the United Nations and an ambassador for health and human trafficking. Dr. Allen is also the historian and secretary for Sisters 4 Sisters Network Inc., the vice president of American Mother's Inc., and on the board of directors of several organizations, including the Eleanor Foundation and Felicia's Fund.

Dr. Allen is a proud and highly decorated twenty-two-year Veteran who served two presidents of the United States on the METU Mayo Clinic team. Featured in the second edition of Who's Who in Black Washington, DC, as one of the "Women of Excellence," she is a bestselling author of *Rebel Rising* and is writing her first solo book, *Star Power.* She is a very proud mother of one amazing son, Chase Joseph.

To connect, email her at ReneeAllenandFriends@gmail.com

Mark T. Gibson is the senior pastor of Redeeming Love Missionary Baptist Church of Raleigh, North Carolina. Born and educated in Washington, DC, he holds a BA in political science from Johnson C. Smith University, an MA in student personnel services from Indiana University of Pennsylvania, and an MDiv from Shaw University. He is currently working on his DMin in pastoral leadership at Campbell University.

After thirty-two years of service as a student affairs professional, Rev. Gibson retired from higher education. He is the loving husband of Margo Rice Gibson; the proud father of four sons, the late Mark Thomas Gibson II, Lamont Junious, Myles Tyler, and Matthew Trenton ("Trent"), and one daughter, Chelsey; the grandfather to Malachi Joshua and Nola Grace; and the fourth of five sons: Philip, David, Bernie, and his identical twin brother, the late Paul Elliot Gibson.

To connect, email him at eldermarkgibson@yahoo.com

Lee R. Jackson is an anxiety coach, mindset mentor, inspirational speaker, and the author of *BOLD EXTRAORDINARY YOU: The 18 Essential Mindsets for Living Life to the Fullest and Becoming the Best Version of Yourself.*

Learn more at https://boldextraordinaryyou.com

Charles Louis Lee Jr. is a skilled mental health service provider who has served the Washington, DC, metropolitan community for more than twenty years. Born in Washington, DC, and raised predominantly by his single mother, Charles was educated by the DC public school system and attended the University of Maryland, College Park to study emergency medical care.

Charles currently serves as a mental health residential counselor for an assigned group of chronically ill and medically compromised mental health consumers living in the community. Prior to this role, Charles served as a mental health counselor and behavioral health technician, working a combined fifteen years for the DC Department of Behavioral Health in acute psychosis and chronic illness stabilization. Charles also served as a nonclinical manager for HCA Dominion Hospital and as a safety coordinator for HCA Northern Virginia Community Hospital.

Adonicca MeChelle is a native North Carolinian whose core values are kindness, progress, and authenticity. With over ten years of dedication in public service, advocacy, and legal response, she works to develop resources and support programs for victims of domestic and gender-based violence, as well as other crimes, across the state. Adonicca is a graduate of the Sociology and Criminology Department of the University of North Carolina Wilmington, and holds a master of public administration from the Rutgers University School of Public Affairs and Administration.

Jacinth McAllister is an overcomer who used counseling and prayer to overcome mental and emotional trauma. Jacinth hopes her transparency and triumph over grief, low self-esteem, self-doubt, and disappointment will encourage others to seek treatment for their own traumas and live mentally and emotionally healthy lifestyles.

Jacinth earned an associate's degree in business from Johnston Community College and has been employed with the State of North Carolina for sixteen years. Her love of fashion jewelry and positive message t-shirts led her into entrepreneurship, and she owns and operates JAMzSpot, a custom bead jewelry and t-shirt company.

In her spare time, Jacinth enjoys reading, traveling, spending time with family and friends, and volunteering with local nonprofit organizations geared toward helping teenage mothers. She resides in Garner, North Carolina, and has one son, Jalon, who is attending Fayetteville State University.

To connect, email her at JMcAllister24@gmail.com

Doris Beasley Haynes-Mullings is an ordained minister, a motivational speaker, a mentor, a life coach, a credit repair agent, and the ninth child of the late Clarence and Matilda Beasley. She graduated from Franklin High School in Franklin, Virginia, and later earned her bachelor's degree from the New Jersey Evangelical Bible Institute in Newark, New Jersey. Doris worked in affirmative action and conducted workshops to bringing about consciousness. She has moderated or conducted Bible studies both in classrooms and virtually.

To connect, email her at dorisinstructor@yahoo.com

Jennifer Norman is a US Marine Corps Veteran and former deputy sheriff from North Carolina. She has a bachelor's in business and numerous certifications from her time in the military, with the sheriff's department, and as a residential manager at a home for intellectually disabled adults. Jennifer traveled the world for work but now finds the joy in traveling for fun after her retirement. Jennifer was first introduced to the mental health world during her time in the Marines. She has found strength in sharing her story with other women, providing hope to women veterans by helping them realize they are not alone.

Jennifer currently resides in Northern Virginia with her spouse of nineteen years, an incredibly special "able" bonus family member, and her two dogs. She is a mother of two adult females and a grandmother to four.

To connect, email her at Jennifer.norman@comcast.net

Rosetta Marie Price is a native Washingtonian. She is a mother to one daughter, Angela, and a grandmother to two grandchildren. Rosetta was educated in DC public schools before earning a bachelor's degree in administrative justice from the University of District of Columbia and her master's degree in mental health counseling from Bowie State University.

Rosetta has been working with the DC Department of Behavioral Health as a first responder in the Community Response Team for twelve years. She serves the community by providing support to individuals who may need hospitalization for mental health episodes such as psychosis, severe self-harm, or suicide attempts. Rosetta is an active member of her church, Southeast Christian Fellowship. When she's not dedicating her time to serving those with mental health concerns, Rosetta enjoys spending time with family, shopping, and keeping up with fashion trends.

To connect, email her at rm_price0428@yahoo.com

Denise M. Simmons is a professor of business management and administration at Northern Virginia Community College in the DMV area. She has held several leadership roles at the community college, including discipline chair, dual enrollment liaison, and steering committee chair. Professor Simmons has been teaching at the community college since 2002. She currently is a doctoral student at Liberty University all but dissertation (ABD) and is in the process of research for her dissertation applied project.

Professor Simmons is a published author for an academic textbook. She has also coauthored an article in a professional journal. Professor Simmons has two children, one in college and the other in high school.

To connect, email her at deesimmons777@gmail.com

La Kia M. Smith, LICSW, works for the DC Department of Behavioral Health CPEP as well as the DC VAMC. Previously, she worked as a clinical supervisor at DC Coalition for the Homeless and served as a social worker at Child and Family Services Agency and Walter Reed AMC. La Kia served five years in the US Army as a medical laboratory technician and autopsy apprentice before she was honorably discharged and medically retired. She then served as a cochair of the Social Justice Committee for the NASW, DC Metro Chapter, as well as a board member for a nonprofit organization that works with ex-offenders and reentry in the DC metro area.

La Kia received her BA in sociology from Paine College and her MSW from the Catholic University of America. She also completed the Certified Addiction Counselor and Dialectical Behavioral Therapy (DBT) certifications.

To connect, email her at lakiasmith.lms@gmail.com

Lashonia Thompson-El holds a bachelor's degree in human relations, and she is the author of *Through the WIRE: My Search for Redemption.* She is the executive director of the WIRE: Women Involved in Reentry Efforts (www.thewiredc.org) and the cochief of violence reduction at the DC Office of the Attorney General. Lashonia is the proud wife of Sean Thompson-El, and together, they have thirteen grandchildren.

To connect, email her at Lashonia.thewire@gmail.com

Sean Thompson-El holds a master's degree in criminology, law, and justice with a concentration in violent studies from the University of Illinois at Chicago. Sean works as a community mental health specialist for the District of Columbia. He works, volunteers, and mentors. He is an advocate for mental health awareness and against gun violence. Sean is married to Lashonia Thompson-El, and together, have thirteen grandchildren. They live and work in Washington, DC.

To connect, email him at seanthomel.thewire@gmail.com

Michael Young is a lifelong Washingtonian, a graduate of DeMatha Catholic High School, and a graduate of TESST Electronics. After high school, Mr. Young joined the United States Marine Corps, where he was promoted meritoriously on several occasions, ultimately reaching the grade of E-4 (Corporal) before receiving an honorable discharge.

Mr. Young applied for the Department of Mental Health's Certified Peer Specialist Program and began working for the Department of Behavioral Health's Mobile Crisis Service doing crisis work. He has also worked with the Department of Corrections's RSAT Program.

Mr. Young has the full support of his family as he maintains good mental and physical health and helps others to do so as well. Mr. Young is married to Certified Lay Minister Romain Young and resides in Northwest Washington, DC.

Anthony Jerome McAllister is a husband, father, and Q-Pop to his grandson, Zyir. He is a dedicated father and husband and has been happily married to his lovely and incredibly supportive wife, Tyreese, for the past twenty-eight years.

Anthony is a leader in the communities of Alexandria, Virginia, and Prince George's County, Maryland, and has served the City of Alexandria for the past twenty-eight years as a juvenile probation/parole officer. An ordained deacon, and a proud thirty-three-year member of Omega Psi Phi Fraternity, Inc., Anthony was appointed to the Prince George's County, Maryland, Commission for Fathers, Men and Boys. He and his wife are the owners of Clinical and Forensic Associates, a private mental health practice and consulting firm located in Upper Marlboro, Maryland, and the cofounders of The Ayana J. McAllister Legacy Foundation.

Learn more at anthonymcallister.com

CREATING DISTINCTIVE BOOKS
WITH INTENTIONAL RESULTS

We're a collaborative group of creative masterminds
with a mission to produce high-quality books to position
you for monumental success in the marketplace.

Our professional team of writers, editors, designers,
and marketing strategists work closely together to ensure
that every detail of your book is a clear representation
of the message in your writing.

Want to know more?
Write to us at info@publishyourgift.com
or call (888) 949-6228

Discover great books, exclusive offers, and more at
www.PublishYourGift.com

Connect with us on social media

@publishyourgift

CPSIA information can be obtained
at www.ICGtesting.com
Printed in the USA
JSHW010135040922
29963JS00002B/9

9 781644 843352